CELEBRATING 54 YEARS AT

FREEDOM HALL

GREAT EVENTS AND MEMORABLE MOMENTS AT ONE OF AMERICA'S PREMIER ARENAS

CELEBRATING 54 YEARS AT

FREEDOM HALL

GREAT EVENTS AND MEMORABLE MOMENTS AT ONE OF AMERICA'S PREMIER ARENAS

BY BILLY REED

Published by

The Kentucky State Fair Board

in partnership with

BUTLER BOOKS
LOUISVILLE

ISBN 978-1-935497-11-0
Printed in Canada

Unless otherwise noted, the photographs and other images contained in this
book were provided by the Kentucky State Fair Board.

Dustjacket and Contents page photographs provided by: *The Courier-Journal*,
University of Louisville Sports Information, University of Kentucky Audio-Visual
Archives, Chris Hall, Doug Shiflet, and the Kentucky State Fair Board.

Book design by Scott Stortz

Published by:

Kentucky State Fair Board
P.O. Box 37130
Louisville, KY 40233
(502) 367-5000

www.kyexpo.org

in partnership with:

Butler Books
P.O. Box 7311
Louisville, KY 40207
(502) 897–9393
Fax (502) 897–9797

www.butlerbooks.com

ACKNOWLEDGMENTS

I have no idea how many basketball games, concerts, and other events I've covered in Freedom Hall over the last five decades, but I thoroughly enjoyed revisiting many of them while doing this book. Much to my surprise, however, photographs were harder to come by than I had expected going in. So I had to send out an S.O.S. to a lot of friends, old and new, to dig into their files.

Many of the photos in the Kentucky Colonels and State Tournament chapters were provided by Lloyd "Pink" Gardner, whom I met when he was a student manager for the Western Kentucky University basketball teams in the 1960s. He went on to become the trainer for the Colonels and a state-championship coach at Fairdale High.

I also depended heavily on Kenny Klein, the associate senior athletics director for sports information at the University of Louisville; Bill Straus, the outstanding freelance photographer from Lexington; Kenny Trivette, the son of legendary Pikeville High coach John Bill Trivette and a successful coach in his own right; Charlie Ruter, the veteran international track-and-field official and Freedom Hall scorekeeper; and Brian Moore, who photographed several events for me when I was executive director of communications for the Kentucky Commerce Cabinet.

Three of my former employers – *The Courier-Journal, Sports Illustrated,* and *The Lexington Herald-Leader* – were uncommonly generous in allowing us to reprint photographs, newspaper clippings and magazine covers. I thank them not only for that, but for giving me the opportunity to represent them in press boxes across America.

When I first came up with the idea for the book, I took it to Harold Workman, the president and CEO of the Kentucky State Fair Board. He's one of the most competent and effective leaders I've ever been around, so I was thrilled when he authorized the project and gave me the go-ahead to line up Butler Books for the layout, design, and printing.

Although she still was grieving from the death of her husband Bill, who founded Butler Books in 1989, Carol Butler took on the project and, with the help of Billy Butler and Elizabeth Sawyer, did her usual excellent job of pulling all the parts together. I was thrilled when she retained Scott Stortz to do the design work because, for my money, he's the best around.

I hired Mark Coomes, longtime friend and former colleague of the author, to pick out the photographs for all the basketball chapters. He also wrote many of the captions and provided ideas that were invaluable. Edward Browne of the State Fair Board staff also assisted in that capacity.

On their behalf and mine, I thank Amy Innskeep of *The Courier-Journal* library; Scarlett Mattson of the World's Championship Horse Show; and DeWayne Peevey and the University of Kentucky sports archives. Your patience and help was greatly appreciated.

Finally, I want to thank those family members and friends who provided special encouragement – Rob, Amy, Caroline and Lucy Frederick; Susan Reed; Bill Malone, Jim Host, Tom Jurich, Gene Thompson, Bob Stallings, Martha McMahon, Leon Middleton, and others to whom I apologize in advance for overlooking.

I only hope this book, in a small way, revives a lot of fond memories of the historic and unforgettable events that have made Freedom Hall a part of all our lives.

– Billy Reed, Louisville, Ky.

CONTENTS

13 Foreword

19 "The Most Beautiful Auditorium in the World"

31 The Sweet Sixteen

43 World's Championship Horse Show

57 The Final Fours

71 Concerts for all Musical Tastes

83 The Kentucky Colonels and the ABA

97 The Toughest Ticket in Sports

103 UK's Home Away From Home

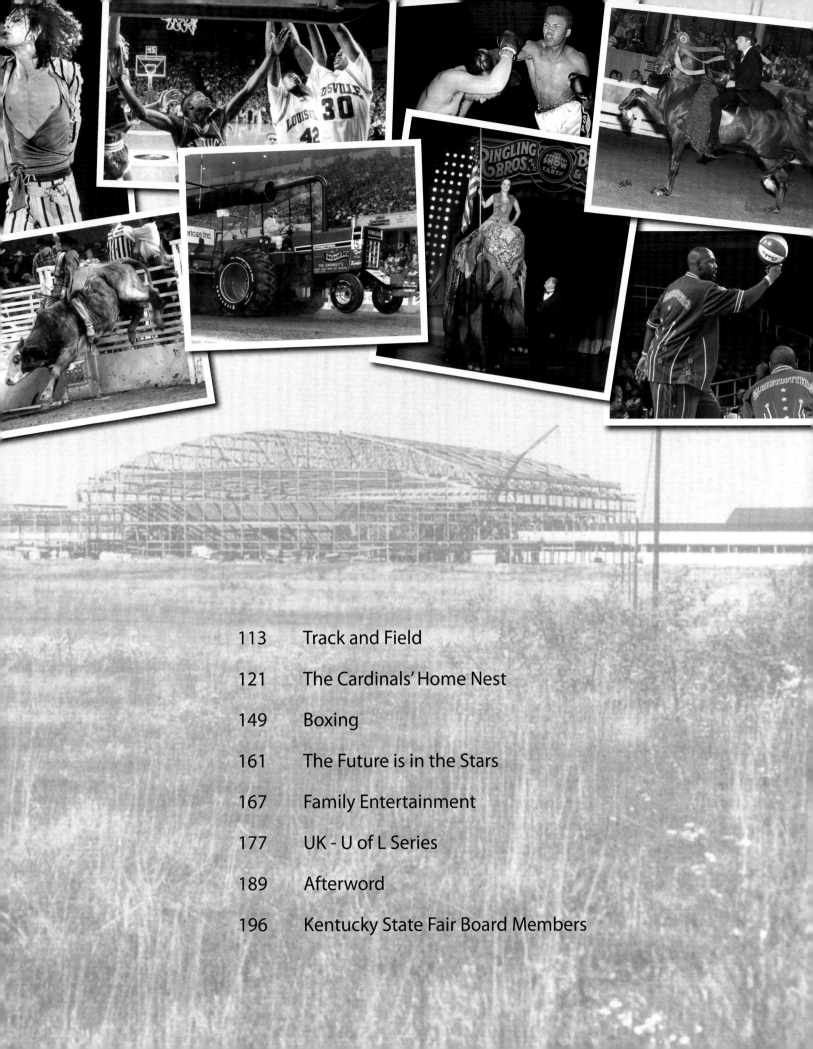

113 Track and Field

121 The Cardinals' Home Nest

149 Boxing

161 The Future is in the Stars

167 Family Entertainment

177 UK - U of L Series

189 Afterword

196 Kentucky State Fair Board Members

STEVEN L. BESHEAR
GOVERNOR

700 CAPITOL AVENUE
SUITE 100
FRANKFORT, KY 40601
(502) 564-2611
FAX: (502) 564-2517

Dear Friends:

Each visit made to the famed Freedom Hall reminds visitors of the many events that have taken place during its rich history. As part of the Kentucky Exposition Center, it has successfully brought millions of visitors, thousands of shows and hundreds of millions of dollars in economic impact to Louisville and the Commonwealth of Kentucky.

Events such as the Kentucky State Fair, which encompasses the World's Championship Horse Show; the North American International Livestock Exposition, which features the North American Championship Rodeo; and the National Farm Machinery Show and its Championship Tractor Pull have become synonymous with Freedom Hall.

Each year it is also home to numerous concerts, conventions, family shows, sporting events and other performances. Attractions such as the National Quartet Convention, the National Square Dance Convention, the National Street Rod Association Street Rod Nationals, FFA's national convention, the Harlem Globetrotters, and concerts such as AC/DC and John Mayer will showcase the arena's capability to continue hosting quality future events. It is truly one of the greatest assets to tourism in the Commonwealth.

As you journey through Freedom Hall's traditions and celebrated moments and look to its future, I hope you feel the pride this facility brings to the Bluegrass State. I would like to extend a heartfelt thank you to the Kentucky State Fair Board for showcasing the facility's successes. I look forward to all the new endeavors, achievements and memories that Freedom Hall will generate in the years to come.

Sincerely,

Steven L. Beshear

Steven L. Beshear

Kentucky State Fair Board

Dear Friends,

We are delighted to have this opportunity to celebrate the past traditions, the many firsts and the joys that Freedom Hall brought and continues to bring to millions of visitors since first opening its doors in 1956. Throughout Freedom Hall's 54-year history, it has hosted many highlighted events for Louisville and the Commonwealth of Kentucky. To name a few, famed boxer Muhammad Ali made his professional boxing debut as Cassius Clay in 1960 in Freedom Hall. The Rolling Stones, Elvis, Cher, Michael Jackson and Taylor Swift have all packed the arena with fans since the 1960s. Future President John F. Kennedy held a political rally within its walls in 1958.

As we look to the future of Freedom Hall, we cannot ignore its celebrated equine past. When the arena was originally designed, its main purpose was for hosting the Kentucky State Fair Horse Show. This purpose continues to be honored with the World's Championship Horse Show, held in conjunction with the Kentucky State Fair each August. The equine industry embraces Freedom Hall as one of the best horse show facilities in the nation and pours millions of dollars into Louisville's economy each year with this annual event.

One of the most well-known traditions of Freedom Hall is the University of Louisville men's and women's basketball programs. They will be moving to their new home, the Louisville Arena, at the end of the 2009-2010 season. As this era comes to an end, it allows us the chance to reflect and realize the opportunity that Freedom Hall offered to the Cardinals to become one of the nation's premier NCAA basketball programs and to grow into a powerhouse of the Big East Conference. Along with thousands of Cardinal home games throughout the years, Freedom Hall also hosted numerous "Battle of the Bluegrass" games between in-state rivals the University of Louisville and the University of Kentucky, state high school championship basketball tournaments and Adolph Rupp's 1958 University of Kentucky NCAA Championship game.

We are truly blessed, thrilled and excited at what Freedom Hall has accomplished. As we look to the future, we are reminded that Freedom Hall is a key element in the Kentucky Exposition Center's status as a top ten public facility in the nation, and we are eager for the successes it will continue to bring to Louisville and the Commonwealth.

Sincerely,

Mr. Harold Workman
President and CEO
Kentucky State Fair Board

Mr. Lanny Greer
Chairman
Kentucky State Fair Board

P.O. Box 37130 • Louisville, Kentucky 40233.7130 • 502.367.5000 • FAX 502.367.5109
www.kyexpo.org • www.kyconvention.org

An Equal Opportunity Employer M/F/D

FOREWORD

I must begin this ode to Freedom Hall by telling about the time Elvis Presley kissed the mother of my children. It was in 1976, and, believe it or not, I literally had to beg her to accept a front-row ticket to an Elvis concert. (I got it courtesy of my friend A.C. Chapman, who then was helping Don Johnston run Freedom Hall.) She had been a music major in college and sung in choirs all her life, so her idea of good popular music pretty much began and ended with, oh, John Denver. But I nagged her until she finally consented to go see Elvis. I think I convinced her to forget about the music and, instead, regard it as a cultural experience.

I left her at her seat and went backstage to watch the concert from there. Every Elvis concert was more or less the same, so about halfway through, he put some scarves around his neck and began strolling back-and-forth across the front of the stage, an invitation for the screaming women up front to charge. Smiling, Elvis would then kneel and reach into the sea of clutching arms and screaming maniacs to put a scarf around a lucky woman's neck and pull her toward him to give her a kiss.

Well, you can imagine my shock when I saw the mother of my children right there in the middle of the howling pack. And doggoned if Elvis didn't single her out – he always picked out the prettiest ones – and pull her toward him for a big smooch. Later in this book you will find a photograph of just such a moment. I don't think the woman in the picture is the mother of my daughters, but I'm not sure. The thing is, it certainly could be. And so, right there in front of my eyes, did Elvis steal her heart.

From that day forward, John Denver never had a chance.

Of all the hours I've spent in Freedom Hall, of all the many different events I've covered there since 1960, of all the incredible memories I have of games and concerts and even the Tractor Pull, this is one of the best.

But we all have Freedom Hall memories, don't we? During the building's 54-year existence, virtually every Kentuckian – and millions of visitors from around the world – have been there for something or the other. As the centerpiece of the Kentucky Exposition Center, Freedom Hall, over the years, has really become our old Kentucky home, hasn't it? It's one of the few places where Kentuckians of all ages, races, religions and socio-economic backgrounds can mix comfortably. It belongs as much to the rural folks who flock to the State Fair every August as to the Jefferson Countians who go there to support the Louisville Cardinals basketball team.

Some may think it's foolish to get sentimental over a building. Yet, Freedom Hall is more than just another collection of bricks and mortar. We have laughed and cried together at Freedom Hall. We have witnessed great victories and suffered bitter defeats. We have been mesmerized by the words and deeds and music of the best our society has to offer. We have watched our sons and daughters graduate. We have shared experiences that have touched and shaped our lives, never to be forgotten.

So although U of L basketball games will move to the new downtown arena in the fall of 2010, all those who regard Freedom Hall as special are luckier than those who have witnessed the wrecking ball destroy such hallowed public buildings as the original Yankee Stadium in New York, Crosley Field and Riverfront Stadium in Cincinnati, the Boston Gardens, Chicago Stadium and the Seattle Kingdome. Freedom Hall will still be around to be the home of concerts, the World's Championship Horse Show, the Tractor Pull, some family-entertainment events and even some basketball games. It will continue to be an important part of our community and our culture.

Through more than five decades, the growth of the Fairgrounds complex has been astonishing. Originally, it consisted of an arena with connecting exhibition wings on either side and a stadium for baseball, football and concerts. Today the complex has grown and expanded to the point that it bears scant resemblance to its original form. Still, Freedom Hall and the wings have remained connected, giving the complex more space under one roof than any similar complex in the nation. From 2002 through early 2009, more than six million customers had come to Freedom Hall for one reason or another.

In the Commonwealth of Kentucky's history, no arena has served the public so well, on so many levels, for so long. This is a tribute to the visionaries who planned the Kentucky State Fairgrounds complex and saw it through to completion…to the members of the State Fair board who have served so admirably as trustees of the public good… and to the executive directors and staff personnel who have worked tirelessly to book the events and make certain they are conducted in the professional manner that has made Freedom Hall one of the most respected names in the sports and entertainment world.

During my days at *The Courier-Journal*, I always felt the newspaper should assign a beat reporter to the Fairgrounds because it was a small city unto itself, one where something interesting and newsworthy was always happening. Everybody knew about the basketball games and the concerts, of course,

but what about all the conventions, the knife-and-gun shows and the flea markets? Sometimes they got covered, sometimes not. But every one brought countless visitors to Louisville, and every one produced business stories, news stories and human-interest stories.

Denny Crum and the author before a game

My personal Freedom Hall inventory includes one of the six Final Fours held there (1967); scores of U of L basketball games under coaches Peck Hickman, John Dromo, Denny Crum, and Rick Pitino; just about every one of the boys' state high school basketball tournaments held there from 1957 through 1994; numerous concerts ranging from Neil Diamond to George Strait; one political convention (the American Party, 1972); and heaven only knows how many other events, ranging from the World's Championship Horse Show to the Harlem Globetrotters.

Once, as you will read later in this book, Loretta Lynn invited me to join her after a concert in the huge motor home she had parked in the Freedom Hall parking lot. While her husband snored, we stayed up until the wee hours, talking about her incredible rise from young mountain mama in Butcher Holler to international country-music icon.

And I shouldn't forget the Kentucky Colonels of the late, great ABA.

I was there the night that Wendell Ladner, the Colonels' resident sex symbol and Burt Reynolds look-alike, ran his arm through a glass water cooler, causing a gash that had female hearts throbbing all over the city. I was there just about every time Julius "Dr. J" Erving came to town because he was the game's greatest showman this side of Pistol Pete Maravich. And I was there the day the Colonels beat the hated Indiana Pacers to wrap up the 1975 championship and give Kentucky its only major professional championship team in any sport.

The Colonels' Hubie Brown has to be in any conversation about the best coach ever to work the sidelines in Freedom Hall. Other candidates include John Wooden of UCLA (who won two of his 10 NCAA titles in Freedom Hall), Adolph Rupp of Kentucky (whose "Fiddlin' Five" won the 1958 national title in Freedom Hall), Dean Smith of North Carolina (whose first Final Four team played in the 1967 event at Freedom Hall), Bob Knight of Indiana (who played for Ohio State in the 1962 Final Four at Freedom Hall) and, of course, resident geniuses Hickman and Crum. And we can't leave out Rick Pitino, the only man to coach both UK and U of L and the first to take three different programs to the Final Four.

As his 2009-2010 U of L team prepared for the program's final season in Freedom Hall, Pitino sounded a bit wistful.

"I love Freedom Hall," he said. "It's like Wrigley Field or Fenway Park. It's an institution. It's always been a great place to play basketball and still is. We're looking forward to the new place, but we're going to miss Freedom Hall."

I would be remiss if I didn't mention the ink-stained wretches and radio-TV announcers with whom I've shared the press table at Freedom Hall since 1962, when I covered the state tournament in which Mike Silliman's St. Xavier team defeated Larry Conley's Ashland Tomcats for the championship. Conley, of course, would return to Freedom Hall many times – first to play for the UK Wildcats

(1963-1966) and later as a TV analyst for ESPN and other networks.

One of my all-time favorite people, Al McGuire, coached at Freedom Hall when he was at Marquette and then frequently worked there as part of the best college hoops announcing team ever assembled – Dick Enberg, Billy Packer, and McGuire, who teamed up for NBC in the late 1970s and early '80s. Anytime Al had an assignment in Louisville, he always would check to see if there was a flea market going on at the Fairgrounds. He was an avid collector of toy soldiers and anything else that struck his fancy. He took me with him a couple of times, and I still have some sheet music he bought for me because the song had something to do with Kentucky.

Brian Moore

First Lady Glenna Fletcher, Dick Vitale, Kentucky Governor Ernie Fletcher (2005).

At one time or another, all the best national radio and TV announcers have worked in Freedom Hall. The list includes names like Curt Gowdy, Chris Schenkel, Jim McKay, and Dick Vitale. But none were any better than some of the voices that were born and/or bred in Kentucky.

Van Vance, a former Western Kentucky University basketball player, was the radio voice of both the Kentucky Colonels and the University of Louisville. He was succeeded by Paul Rogers, a native of Louisville, who graduated from the University of Kentucky and learned the business from Cawood Ledford at WHAS radio and TV in the early 1970s.

Ledford today is regarded as maybe the best college basketball play-by-play man ever, but in the 1950s and '60s, some contended that he wasn't even the best in Kentucky. He and Claude Sullivan were friendly competitors, Ledford working the games for 50,000-watt WHAS in Louisville and Sullivan doing them for the Standard Oil network and its flagship station, WVLK in Lexington.

Both were so good that even though Bernie Shively, then the UK athletics director, wanted to establish a single network with one "voice of the Wildcats," he refused to pick between them. His dilemma was resolved, sadly, when Sullivan died of throat cancer in 1967.

During his career as sports director at WHAS, Ledford worked more than UK games. He called some U of L games in Freedom Hall, and even did some state tournaments. In 1959, after California had won the NCAA championship in Freedom Hall, Ledford was designated to present the winning coach, Pete Newell, with a new range built at General Electric's Appliance Park.

"I ran into Pete years later," Ledford said. "He told me he still had the range and it was working as good as new."

Cawood was succeeded by Tom Leach, who has carried on Cawood's tradition of excellence far better than any coach who succeeded Wooden at UCLA or Bear Bryant at Alabama.

And then there are the scribes, bless their hearts. When Freedom Hall was still in the planning stage, it got the blessing of Earl Ruby, the *Courier-Journal* sports editor

UK not losing 'voice'

Ledford quits WHAS, keeps play-by-play role

Billy Reed
Courier-Journal sports editor

Cawood Ledford leaned back in his office chair and lit what must have been his 24th or 25th cigarette of the day, judging by the ashtray full of stubs on his cluttered desk. "I'm hittin' 'em pretty good today," Ledford said, smiling as he took a drag. "I'm nervous, I guess."

Only a few hours earlier, Ledford had walked into the office of his boss, Bob Morse, and dropped a bombshell — his resignation as sports director of WHAS radio and television. He plans to open a new company, Cawood Ledford Productions, in Lexington.

The new venture won't affect Ledford's role as play-by-play announcer for the University of Kentucky Wildcats, at least for the foreseeable future. His new business partner, Lexington entrepreneur Jim Host, is in the second year of a three-year contract that gives him exclusive broadcast rights to UK football and basketball games.

In interviews yesterday, Ledford and Host both emphasized that the 53-year-old announcer's move wasn't motivated by any unhappiness with his role at WHAS.

"He's had a great relationship with WHAS," Host said, "but over the last four or five years he's become not only a Kentucky and a regional figure, but a national one as well. Doing this gives him much more freedom to do things on a national basis than he had at WHAS."

For example, Host also owns the national radio rights to the semifinals and finals of the NCAA basketball tournament, and he recently signed a three-year contract with NBC to co-produce the radio broadcast of the semifinals and finals. That alliance, Host says, will enable him to put together "the biggest independent network ever to call a sports event in this country."

Host wanted Ledford to be his play-by-play man because "I think he's the best basketball announcer in the country." However, WHAS wouldn't allow Ledford to call the NCAA for Host because NBC's Louisville affiliate is WAVE, its leading rival. Now, however, Ledford is free to call this year's semifinals and finals in Salt Lake City — pro-vided UK doesn't make the Final Four. The NCAA doesn't permit a team's play-

See LEDFORD
Page 5, Col. 1, this section

Cawood Ledford, leaving WHAS for a new venture in Lexington, will continue to call play-by-play action at University of Kentucky games.
Staff Photo

Reprinted with permission from *The Courier-Journal*

who was a friend and sometime hunting buddy of various Kentucky governors and other political big shots. Dean Eagle, as sports editor of *The Louisville Times*, arranged the 1966 game in which native son Silliman's senior team at Army came to Freedom Hall to play Wes Unseld's sophomore team at U of L. (The Army coach then was Knight, only four years removed from his 1962 Final Four appearance in Freedom Hall with Ohio State).

Besides Ruby and Eagle, Louisville has been blessed with an abundance of talented sports writers. I hesitate to mention names, because I'm sure to leave out many, but I'd be remiss if I didn't mention Dave Kindred, Dick Fenlon, and Mike Barry, whose columns graced the Louisville sports pages from the late 1960s through the '70s...Earl Cox, the greatest media ally that Kentucky high school sports have ever had and the guy who ran the combined *Courier-Journal* and *Louisville Times* sports department for more than a decade...Rick Bozich, sports columnist at the *Times* and/or *C-J* from 1981 to the present... columnists Pat Forde, Jerry Brewer, and Eric Crawford...and gifted reporters such as Johnny Carrico, Tev Laudeman, Jim Terhune, Mike Sullivan, John McGill, Jr., Russ Brown, Jim Bolus, and Stan Sutton.

Back in the day, U of L put the *Courier*'s seats right next to the Cards' bench, which turned many of us, myself included, into eaves-droppers. I never could figure out how Crum could yell at his players and chew gum at the same time. I never saw him lose the gum at Freedom Hall, but I did one time at Mid-South Coliseum in Memphis. When he

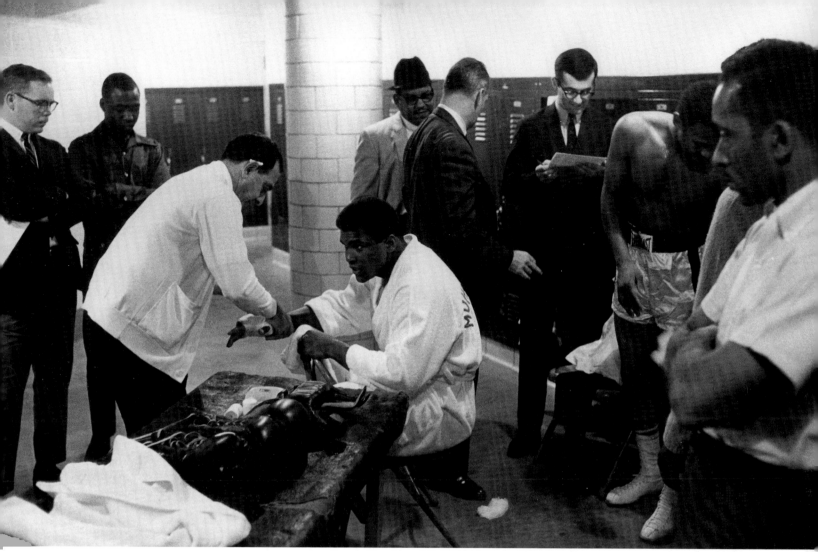

Courier-Journal writers Dave Kindred (left) and Billy Reed (third from right) in Muhammad Ali's dressing room (1966).

thought nobody was looking, he went on the floor, picked it up and put it back in his mouth. Immediately, there came this bellow from behind the bench: "Aw, real nice, Crum!"

I've also sat virtually elbow-to-elbow in Freedom Hall with well-known national writers such as Frank Deford, Peter Carry, and Alex Wolff of *Sports Illustrated*…John Feinstein and Michael Wilbon of *The Washington Post*…Furman Bisher of *The Atlanta Journal-Constitution*…Bob Ryan and Lesley Visser of *The Boston Globe*…Si Burick and Ritter Collett of the *Dayton Daily News*…Dick "Hoops" Weiss and Mike Lupica of the *New York Daily News*…Bob Hammel of the *Bloomington Herald-Times*…Hubert Mizell of the *St. Petersburg Times*…and Dick Joyce of the *Associated Press*.

I'll close by telling you about Muhammad Ali.

He never had a title fight in Louisville, but he began his career in Freedom Hall, as you shall see in the boxing chapter, and he came back in 1966 to fight an exhibition match against Jimmy Ellis, his longtime friend and former sparring partner. Earl Cox assigned Dave Kindred and me to cover the event and, blessedly, a *Courier-Journal* photographer snapped some photos of us in the locker room, talking with the fighters as they got taped up. Looking at the photo, you probably will not recognize us. Jeez. Were we ever really that young and that thin? Ali autographed a photo for me that night and I still have it hanging in my home. The inscription says, "To Billy, Muhammad Ali, World Champ 1966."

Personally, I think that's better than a kiss from Elvis. But, then, I guess it depends on your perspective.

KENTUCKY FAIR
AND
EXPOSITION CENTER
WELCOME
BILLY GRAHAM CRUSADE
COLISEUM
WELCOME

"THE MOST BEAUTIFUL AUDITORIUM IN THE WORLD"

"Good evening, ladies and gentlemen, and WELCOME to the Kentucky Fair and Exposition Center, and Freedom Hall, for the thrill and the excitement of college basketball."

- Longtime Freedom Hall announcer John Tong

When it opened in 1956, the complex at the new Kentucky State Fairgrounds was introduced to America by a man wearing a bowtie and a chimpanzee wearing clothes. The bowtie belong to Dave Garroway, host of the NBC television network's popular *Today* show. He was so impressed by the size and scope of the facilities that he described it as "beautiful," and said, "You have to see it to believe it." His hairy sidekick, J. Fred Muggs, screeched and stuck out his tongue, as was his wont, and generally seemed to feel right at home in the Commonwealth's late-summer tropical heat.

The Kentucky State Fairgrounds complex rises from a meadow.

The grand opening took place on September 7, only four months after jockey Dave Erb had guided Needles to a ¾-length victory over Bill Hartack and Calumet Farm's Fabius in the 82nd Kentucky Derby. Although nobody could have predicted it at the time, the arena at the Fairgrounds, which came to be named Freedom Hall, would join Churchill Downs, home of the Derby, on the very short list of American sporting shrines.

That notion would have drawn a snort of derision from A.B. "Happy" Chandler, the former U.S. Senator and baseball commissioner who was early in his second term as governor when the Fairgrounds was opened. During his winning campaign of 1955, Chandler repeatedly referred to the new Fairgrounds as a "white elephant." Even as the ribbon was being cut at the opening ceremony, Chandler was looking for private investors to take it off the Commonwealth's hands.

This is the same Chandler, of course, who fought his way onto the Freedom Hall court on the night of March 22, 1958, to embrace University of Kentucky basketball coach Adolph Rupp after the Wildcats defeated Seattle to give Rupp his fourth NCAA championship. It was the first of the six NCAA Final Fours that were held in Freedom Hall from then through 1969. No non-dome arena, including New York City's Madison Square Garden, has played host to more.

The truth be told, Chandler's pique over the Fairgrounds probably was due to the fact that he couldn't take any credit

Exterior and interior views of Freedom Hall under construction.

The arena and baseball stadium (foreground) were built with the big leagues in mind.

for it. The plans were laid in 1945 by the State Fair Board and the Louisville Chamber of Commerce. They wanted to build "a grand exposition center unlike any seen south of the Mason-Dixon Line."

The first design was submitted in 1946 by architect Fred Elswich, who sketched his vision of the complex on brown wrapping paper during a Fair Board meeting. The original cost estimate of $2 million turned out to be something of a joke.

Indeed, by the time ground was broken in 1950 by Governor Earle C. Clements, one of Chandler's rivals in the factionalized state Democratic party, the estimate had grown to $6 million and was well on the way to the final cost of around $16 million (as a sign of the changing times, the new downtown arena will cost $238 million in 2009 dollars).

In retrospect, everything about the design and construction of the complex was inspired and visionary. At a time when Americans were more mobile than ever because automobiles had become affordable to the middle class, the new complex was built at what became the intersection of Interstate-65 and the Watterson Expressway, making it easily accessible. It had parking for more than 27,000 cars.

Long before other cities were building sports facilities side-by-side or combining them into multi-purpose

This was how Freedom Hall looked just before the Rev. Billy Graham opened it in 1956.

stadiums, Louisville provided the nation with a glimpse of the future. The centerpiece of the complex was a state-of-the-art arena – or "coliseum," as it was originally known – that connected two huge wings, or pavilions, of exhibition space. The complex also included a 25,000-seat stadium that was deemed to be better than Cincinnati's Crosley Field or other aging major-league baseball parks.

As an indication of how big Louisville was thinking at the time, the first sporting event held in the new stadium was an NFL exhibition game between the Baltimore Colts and the Washington Redskins on Sunday, September 9, 1956. The game was arranged by Bill Henry of Mt. Sterling, who had been hired as a consultant to bring in sporting events. The Colts had a rookie quarterback, Johnny Unitas, who

had played at the University of Louisville. He was to become known as "Mr. Quarterback" as he helped the Colts build an NFL dynasty.

Had the football exhibition been the only game in town, there would have been no problems. But the State Fair also was going on around it, and a record crowd of 90,000 jammed the new site. Unfortunately, only 9,800 of the 27,000 parking spaces had been paved, creating a traffic jam and parking hassle unlike the city had ever seen.

As impressive as the stadium was, however, the coliseum was the crown jewel. Ostensibly, it was built mainly for the Kentucky State Fair World's Championship Horse Show, but the powers-that-be wanted it to be a state-of-the-art, multi-purpose facility that could be adapted for any indoor sport

-- including hockey and track-and-field – and a myriad of other entertainment endeavors including ice shows, circuses, rodeos, political conventions, and religious crusades.

The Rev. Billy Graham called Freedom Hall "the most beautiful auditorium in the world."

Like NBC's Garroway, first-time visitors were inevitably awe-struck over the arena's size and seating capacity. The buzz was similar to what Houston experienced when it opened the Astrodome nine years later. The arena had 14,660 permanent seats that portable bleachers could easily expand to more than 20,000. The first major event held in the coliseum was a Billy Graham Crusade that packed the house.

The arena received Dr. Graham's enthusiastic blessing.

"It is the most beautiful auditorium in the world," he said. "Louisville's new fairgrounds and coliseum offer unlimited potential for our purposes."

Soon after Dr. Graham's crusade, the Kentucky chapter of the American Legion and the State Fair Board announced they were co-sponsoring a contest to name the coliseum. The only criterion was that the building would honor Kentucky's war dead. The winner would receive a $1,000 U.S. Savings Bond and the sponsoring teacher would get $250.

The entries would be judged by a five-man panel that consisted of Dr. Frank G. Dickey, president of UK; Dr. Philip Davidson, president of U of L; Kelly Thompson, president of Western Kentucky State College; Earl Ruby, sports editor of *The Courier-Journal,* and Dean Eagle, sports editor of *The Louisville Times.*

One student, obviously still enthralled by Dr. Graham's crusade, suggested the coliseum be named "Saints Hall" in his honor. But that didn't fit the criterion. Neither did entries such as "The Hub," "Liberatorium," "Derby Coliseum," "Cardinal Memorial Coliseum," or "The Big Top."

Closer to the mark were suggestions such as "Hero Haven," "The Doughboy Coliseum," "The Veterans Coliseum," the "Men-o-War Coliseum," the "Commando Kelly Coliseum," and the "Franklin Sousey Coliseum" in honor of the Kentuckian who was one of the four Marines who raised the American flag on Iwo Jima's Mount Suribachi on February 23, 1945.

After poring over more than 6,500 entries, the judges finally selected "Freedom Hall," which was submitted by Charlotte Owens, 17, a senior at duPont Manual High in Louisville. Here was her winning essay:

Charlotte Owens (right) won the naming contest.

"Freedom…battle cry of the ages! The men who fought for America here and abroad echoed this through the years. Freedom…the essential fiber of being! Dedicating this hall to our Kentucky heroes is but a small service for the great sacrifice they have made for our country's freedom."

The newly-christened arena was dedicated on the night of December 19, 1956, before a crowd of 15,133 that had showed up for a basketball game between Western Kentucky University and defending NCAA champion San Francisco.

Before the game, Charlotte Owens and one of her teachers, Edna Brown, received their prizes from William C. "Speedy" Allen of Marion, vice-commander of the Kentucky American Legion. D.A. Sachs III, chairman of the dedication committee, read a letter from President Dwight D. Eisenhower, the former Army general who had been commander-in-chief of the allied forces in Europe during World War II.

"To the citizens of Kentucky gathered in the dedication of their new Coliseum at the Kentucky Fair and Exposition Center, I send greetings," Eisenhower wrote. "As an expression of respect for your countrymen who gave their lives in the defense of justice and freedom, your Coliseum stands as a noble monument and a promising center for living service. I join you in paying tribute to the heroes of Kentucky, and I congratulate you for the effort and vision required to construct this splendid memorial. Best wishes to you as you enter into the use of your new Coliseum."

For the record, the Hilltoppers defeated San Francisco, 61-57.

In the decades before Freedom Hall was opened, many young Americans worshiped the cowboys they saw at the Saturday matinees in their local movie houses. Their ranks included such names as Gene Autry, Hopalong Cassidy, Bob Gibson, and Ken Maynard. But none was bigger than Roy Rogers, king of the singing cowboys, and his wife, Dale Evans.

So when Roy and Dale appeared at the 1973 State Fair rodeo in Freedom Hall, they were greeted warmly by older fans who remembered simpler and sweeter times in America. Before the show, Rogers did an interview, as he polished off

a banana split piled high with whipped cream.

"Today, if you don't load up a movie with sex and violence, people won't go see it," Rogers said. "You can't tell the good guys from the bad guys, and sometimes the ones you think are good turn out to be bad. Back in our era, right always won out over wrong, and you didn't see a lot of killing and bloodshed. We'd catch 'em and whip the dickens out of 'em, or else take 'em in so the law could take its course. I think the country needs heroes today."

Willie Nelson: "My heroes have always been cowboys..."

Heroes. That's what Freedom Hall always has been about. It was named in honor of the Kentucky heroes who were killed or wounded in combat. And through the years, night after night, game after show after concert, Freedom Hall has been the place where heroes were made, certified, and cheered.

There have been rodeo heroes, the cowboys in their big hats and tooled leather boots who try to ride or rope or otherwise tame some of the meanest, orneriest steers and buckin' broncos ever put on the face of the earth.

There have been circus heroes making tigers jump through hoops and walking tightropes high above the floor and swinging from one trapeze to another while the mesmerized fans watch, necks craned upward and mouths wide open.

Circuses, clowns, ice hockey and basketball exhibitions: The new arena was capable of hosting a vast array of first-class family entertainment productions.

Ex-UK player Wayne Turner playing for the Globetrotters.

Arena football came to Freedom Hall in the 2000s.

Brian Moore

A mother and son talk to their military hero in Iraq. (2004)

There have been skating heroes, some playing for the hockey teams that called Freedom Hall home, and others doing ballet on ice at the various Ice Capades shows that came through town.

There have been football heroes in the Arena Leagues that had a Louisville franchise in the early part of this decade. Football played in a confined space tended to favor the offense, so the Arena teams lit up the overhanging scoreboard as if it were an old-fashioned pinball machine.

There have been patriotic heroes such as future President John F. Kennedy, who appeared at a 1958 political rally in Freedom Hall, and comedian Bob Hope, who did a 1975 Christmas show in Freedom Hall before yet another trip overseas to entertain our troops.

But at no time in its history did the arena better live up to its name than on December 18, 2004. Before and during the Kentucky-Louisville game, the families of Kentucky troops stationed in Iraq were able to visit with their sons and daughters through a two-way satellite hookup. The project, a joint

LEE CHURCHILL's costume leaves no doubt that she's an enthusiastic backer of Alabama Gov. George C. Wallace for president.

Woman deputy sheriff wants 'Wallace in '76'

By BILLY REED
Courier-Journal Staff Writer

Reprinted with permission from
The Courier-Journal

venture organized by the Freedom Calls Foundation, was billed as "Freedom Calls from Freedom Hall."

Before the tipoff, the crowd of 20,000 and the ESPN broadcasting crew could see the troops on huge TV screens on the overhead scoreboard, and the troops in Iraq could see the crowd cheering them. ESPN analyst Dick Vitale was among those waving to the troops and applauding them.

After the game began, the families of the troops adjourned to a special area in the South Wing so they could visit with their sons and daughters one-on-one.

Although Louisville always has seemed a logical choice for either the Democratic or Republican national political conventions, the only one ever held in Freedom Hall came in 1972, when the American Party took over the arena for four days and nominated Rep. John Schmitz for President and former Air Force General Curtis LeMay for Vice-President. The ticket was a non-factor in the November election, when President Richard Nixon won a landslide victory over Democratic challenger George McGovern.

On the political spectrum, the American Party was even to the right of the Republicans. One of the speakers was Lester Maddox, the segregationist lieutenant governor of Georgia, and some of the delegates professed their admiration for former Alabama Governor George Wallace, who had been paralyzed by an assassin's bullet earlier in the spring.

So throughout their convention, the American Party delegates attacked both Nixon and McGovern, the Republicans and the Democrats, with equal fervor. On Friday, the next-to-last day, they even turned their wrath on Col. Harland Sanders, whose recipe for fried chicken had been turned into an international fast-food chain.

It began when two irate female delegates from Ohio charged up to W.S. Krogdahl of the Kentucky delegation and demanded to know why the American Party didn't get free fried chicken, as the Democrats had at their convention in Miami Beach.

Krogdahl explained that the only reason the Democrats got the free chicken was that John Y. Brown Jr., the chairman of the board of Kentucky Fried Chicken, is a Democrat. But that didn't satisfy the delegates. They told Krogdahl they planned to boycott KFC when they got home.

"Oh, they were hot," Krogdahl told a reporter. "Why, they even put up some signs about it."

Indeed, a check around Freedom Hall revealed these ominous messages:

"The Dems Got It…We Want It…Kentucky Fried Chicken!"

"We Want Kentucky Fried Chicken…Y'all Hear, Colonel?"

Most of the unrest was centered in the Ohio delegation.

"I think chicken isn't good enough for us," said an embittered delegate who refused to give his name. "We should have steak, really. We deserve it."

A female delegate, who also refused to be identified, said: "If you're going to do it for one (convention), you should do

it for all. After all, our convention is right here in Louisville. And we're spending our money here, aren't we?"

Ohio delegate Bob Grace said, "I think Kentucky passed up a golden opportunity here. This was the first national convention for the third party. These people could have gained a lot of good will by giving us some chicken."

But a KFC spokesperson said the company was simply following the lead of the television networks in granting equal time to the major parties. He added that despite Brown's Democratic affiliation, KFC had offered to cater the Republican National Convention in the same way it had the Democratic convention, but the GOP hadn't said whether it would accept the offer.

At the closing session, when one speaker referred to Kentucky as "the home of thoroughbred racing and Kentucky Fried Chicken," the delegates booed lustily. It was duly noted that Col. Sanders, who was prominent at the Democratic convention, did not attend any of the American Party sessions in Freedom Hall.

The reason?

"He's chicken," said one delegate.

Over the years, no one person became more closely associated with Freedom Hall than the late John Tong, who served as the arena's public address announcer from 1960 through his retirement in 1999. As the undisputed "Voice of Freedom Hall," he achieved a sort of celebrity status due to his distinct enunciation and phrasing. Everybody who spent much time in Freedom Hall, including rival coaches and referees, eventually came to impersonate Tong's signature phrases, such as "All exits will be open for outgoing traffic!"

Tong was a perfect fit for a place named Freedom Hall. As a sailor in the Navy during World War II, he was on a ship that was anchored near the U.S.S. Missouri on August 8, 1945. On that day, Army General Douglas MacArthur boarded the Missouri to accept the Japanese surrender that

John Tong's voice became synonymous with Freedom Hall and University of Louisville basketball. His game prepartion was as meticulous as his enunciation.

University of Louisville Sports Information

ended World War II. After the war, Tong returned to his native Louisville and began a sales career that eventually led him to O'Connor and Raque, where he worked 39 years selling office supplies and furniture.

In 39 years as "The Voice of Freedom Hall," Tong never missed a U of L home game. His résumé also includes two NCAA Final Fours (1967 and '69), nine years with the Kentucky Colonels of the ABA, Boys State Tournaments in both Freedom Hall and Rupp Arena, the Mason-Dixon Games, and untold pro exhibitions, NCAA regionals, high-school tournaments, conference tournaments, forgotten "classics," the Kentucky-Indiana All-Star series, and whatever other events required the Tong touch.

After succeeding Adolph Rupp as UK's head basketball coach in 1972, Joe B. Hall began to sense there was something different whenever the Wildcats played in Freedom Hall. He finally figured out what it was. "Why can't we have John Tong do our games in Freedom Hall?" Hall asked writer Earl Cox. "He used to do our games with Notre Dame for Coach Rupp." When Cox told him that UK had started bringing the Rupp Arena announcer with them, Hall was, said Cox, "dismayed."

In both his personal and professional life, Tong was a fussy, fastidious man who needed to have everything just so. He took as much pride in his grooming and appearance as he did in his mellifluous voice, so he always wore a suit and tie. Whenever someone would refer to him as a "P.A. man," Tong would gently, but firmly, say that he preferred to be identified as a "stadium and arena announcer."

Sometimes he was accused of talking too much, but most Freedom Hall fans came to accept the Tong style as part of the building, much like the checkered ceiling or the Kentucky Athletic Hall of Fame plaques on the concourse walls. When a traveling violation was committed, Tong always would say, "Steps called!" Even now, the phrases echo in memory: "And time is OUT on the floor!" Or, "From this point on, BOTH teams will shoot the bonus."

Tong had a distinct philosophy about his job.

"In those early years, we didn't have the tremendous crowds that we have now," said Tong in a 1999 interview. "A regular crowd was about 6,000 to 7,000 fans. We appealed not just to U of L fans, but to everyone who might want to come to the games: visiting salesmen, people coming into town. They might even be from the hometown of the other team. We wanted to show sportsmanship, and we didn't want to insult them. I always thought people didn't come to hear me; they came to see the ball game. I wanted them to enjoy the game, so I never gave them that, 'It's time to rumb-llllllllle' stuff. It's not a rumble, it's a basketball game."

Male High School dominated the state tournament in the early 1970s.

The Courier-Journal

THE SWEET SIXTEEN

In the mean winter of 1957, the Big Sandy River became so swollen with rage that it spilled over its banks and spread misery, devastation, and pain through the streets of Pikeville, the coal-mining town where trouble had long been a way of life. As floods go, even by Eastern Kentucky standards, this one was a doozy. Ask anybody who was there. "We had one of the better gyms in the state," said John Bill Trivette, the basketball coach at Pikeville High. "Truly a beautiful place.

But when the flood came, our gym floor was under four feet of water and our kids, my players, had to roll up their sleeves and help clean up the mess."

In one of the most remarkable sagas in the history of Kentucky high school basketball, the Panthers won their region and advanced to the first state tournament in Freedom Hall. Although they lost to eventual state champion Lexington Lafayette in the semifinals, they still stand as one

Ken Trivette

Lafayette High School's Billy Ray Lickert (center, front row) led the 1957 All-State Tournament Team.

Lafayette High won the 1957 State Tournament (above), but Pikeville High, the team without a home, almost stole the show with its full court press.

of the biggest crowd favorites in the 23 state tournaments played in Freedom Hall from 1957 through 1994. Even in Louisville, the little teams from the rural parts of the state always own the hearts of the fans.

The Pikeville starters all were between 5-foot-11 and 6-3. Their names were Tommy Adkins, Darwin Smith, Harold Lockhart, H.L. Justice, and Larry Phillips. Individually, they weren't impressive. But collectively, they were a white tornado that wreaked as much havoc on the floor as the Big Sandy did on their gym. It was all because of their full-court press, which was as much a novelty in the winter of 1957 as was the idea that black students might be peacefully admitted to Central High in Little Rock, Arkansas.

Trivette, as shrewd a mind as has ever coached basketball in the Commonwealth, had begun doodling with the idea of a press since the night little John's Creek almost upset his team by disrupting his patterns. By the 1956-'57 season, he had the concept perfected and the right personnel to play it.

Players from Pikeville, Eastern and Lafayette pose with a vendor.

"I knew in December that we were going to have to play them sooner or later," said Lafayette Coach Ralph Carlisle. "That's why I began making our starters scrimmage every day against six men, so they would know how to handle their press."

After the flood, every Pikeville game was a road game. The Panthers had no home court so Trivette packed them in a bus and took them to Paintsville, Hindman, Ashland, Whitesburg, or any place that had a dry floor and a good team.

They lost only three games in the regular season — twice to a Flat Gap team built around future college stars Charlie Osborne (Western Kentucky) and Carroll Burchett (University of Kentucky) and once to W. L. Kean's Louisville Central Yellow Jackets, who were hoping to become the first all-black team ever to make the state tournament.

The Panthers avenged the loss to Central in a Freedom Hall double-header played for the benefit of flood relief. In the other game, Lafayette's great Billy Ray Lickert, a future UK star, led the Generals past Louisville Manual.

When the state tournament arrived, Freedom Hall was the new Taj Mahal of basketball arenas – the newest, biggest, and most totally awesome hoops palace in the entire nation. The huge crowds, who came to see the arena as much as the games, rooted Pikeville into the semifinals, where the Panthers finally met tournament favorite Lafayette. The trouble was, Trivette's team was so sick and tired heading into the game that Trivette didn't even let them use their press in the first half.

"We were an awful tired team," Trivette said. "It had been a long, hard season, and, physically, we had run out of gas. The only blessing about playing all our games on the road was that we got to take our washing with us."

Without the press, Pikeville staggered to the locker room down by 14 at halftime. So Trivette did the only thing he could, which was ask them to put on the press and leave their guts on the Freedom Hall floor. Midway through the third quarter, Pikeville was only a point behind and Lafayette was reeling like a punch-drunk fighter.

"His was the best press I've ever seen," Carlisle said years later. "We didn't play too well in the first half because we were expecting the press and didn't get it. I've never seen a press like that one."

Even so, the Generals held on, regrouped, and eventually pulled away to a 70-61 victory that left Trivette feeling philosophical. "Lafayette had a real good player in Lickert," he said. "He could play anywhere on the floor, so he gave us problems. Ralph did a fine job. I would like to have won it very badly, but you don't always get your druthers. I guess we went about as far as we could go."

On Saturday night, Pikeville defeated Russell County for third place before Lafayette, obviously weary from battling the Pikeville press earlier in the day, held on for a 55-52 win over Louisville Eastern in the title game. Lickert led the Generals with 26. The crowd was announced as 18,000, then the largest ever to see a basketball game below the Mason-Dixon Line.

For youngsters around the state, coming to Freedom Hall for some big event – the state fair, the state high school basketball tournament, a concert – became almost a rite of passage. It was the place where backgrounds and lifestyles collided all over the place – in malls and hotels, at dances and parties and, mostly, in the corridors and concourses of Freedom Hall.

"Hey," says a cool dude with an "HC" on his jacket, eyeing a chick with an "A" on her sweater. "Where y'all from? Ashland, I reckon."

"Uh-uh," says the girl, batting her false eyelashes and popping her gum. "Atherton. Right here in town."

The kids came from as far away as Hickman County, a school of 322 students in the western end of the state, and

The Courier-Journal

from as nearby as Male High, only a couple of miles from Freedom Hall. They came from small-town schools like Danville and Madisonville, and big-city schools like Henry Clay in Lexington and Shawnee in Louisville.

In fact, one of the most appealing qualities of the state tournament, then as now, is that it's one of the few places where precocious street kids from Newport can mix with Future Farmers from Lee County, where poor kids from the coal fields near McDowell can rap with socialites from the horse country around Lexington.

But no matter what the size of the school or town, they all have this in common: To look sharp, be cool, stay up all night, outwit parents and chaperones, and – yes! – to seek and find romance amid the temptations of The Big City.

It was an event for the cheerleaders as much as the players.

"We want vic-tor-ee,

"We want vic-tor-ee,

"Hey, hey, hey…"

Somewhere along the line, maybe about the time Mike Casey was leading Shelby County to the 1966 championship, cheerleading ceased to become a matter of just putting the prettiest girls in short skirts and letting them stand out there in front of the crowd, moving their arms or jumping when the spirit moved them.

It became a sort of semi-sport. It became a competition. It even became, heaven help us, co-ed. Strong guys who weren't big or tall enough to play basketball or football became cheerleaders.

So in the 1970s and '80s, while the basketball teams scampered up and down the floor, the cheerleaders went against each other, matching smiles, twirls, whirls, dance numbers, pom-pom routines, booty shakes, and – of course – cheers. We must not forget the cheers, although they sometimes are almost beside the point.

And let's not ignore the mascots.

At the 1973 tournament, Campbellsville High's mascot

The Courier-Journal

Clay County's Tigers were skinned by Ballard, in '88

was a student dressed up in a purple eagle suit, complete with a papier-mâché head. It was the mascot's duty to dance around, lead cheers, and generally whoop it up.

But, say, doesn't it get a little hot in there?

"Boy, I'll say," said Maria Maupin, 15, the sophomore in the suit. "I'm suffocatin' in here."

The Hazard team that lost to Pikeville in the 1957

Coach Adolph Rupp, Larry Conley, Mike Silliman, George Conley (Larry's dad).

state tournament quarterfinals had three African-American players, making it the first "Sweet Sixteen" to be integrated. When the tournament returned to Freedom Hall in 1960, the championship was won by Louisville Flaget, a Catholic school from West Louisville coached by Jim Morris.

Historically, the Braves' most important starter wasn't scoring leaders Tom Finnegan or Ted Deeken, but the guard who joined them on the all-tournament team – John McGill, the first African-American to start for a state championship team. McGill also broke some racial barriers in tennis, where he was a championship-caliber player.

In 1962, another Catholic school from Louisville – St. Xavier – won the championship behind 6-6 center Mike

Silliman, who went on to become an All-American at West Point and the captain of the 1968 U.S. Olympic team that won the gold medal in Mexico City. The Tigers were coached by rookie Joe Reibel, who had inherited the team when Gene Rhodes abruptly quit after the 1961 season.

The '62 title game between St. X and Ashland was the last in which all the players were white. Only a year later, black players dominated the state tournament, earning eight of ten spots on the all-tournament team. The '63 champion, Louisville Seneca, was led by African-Americans Wes Unseld, a bullish 6-6 junior center who threw the most ferocious outlet passes anybody had seen, and Mike Redd, a 6-3 senior guard who was Michael Jordan before there was Michael Jordan.

Central cuts down the nets in 1969.

In the title game, the Redskins defeated Lexington Dunbar, 72-66. The Bearcats, coached by S.T. Roach, still were an all-black school. It was the second time they came up empty in the title game, having also lost to Ashland in 1961. The first historically black school to win the state title was Louisville Central, led by hot-shooting Ron King and the lightning-bug, Otto Petty, in 1969.

To this day, the '63 tournament was arguably the most talented in history. Besides Seneca's Unseld and Redd, the all-tournament team included Clem Haskins of Taylor County; Dwight Smith of Princeton Dotson; Charlie Taylor of Owensboro; George Davis of Maysville, James Smith and George Wilson of Dunbar; Danny Shearer of Oldham County; and Pearl Hicks of Clay County.

Unseld and Haskins went on to become consensus All-Americans at Louisville and Western Kentucky, respectively. Smith, who became Haskins' teammate at Western, would

Wes Unseld (with his parents, left) led Seneca High School to back-to-back titles in 1963-64.

have been a first-round NBA draft pick had he not died in a car accident after his senior year in college. Hicks got a scholarship to Vanderbilt.

The most exciting player of them all, Redd, could have played for any college in the nation, but couldn't qualify academically for a scholarship. He played a year or so at Kentucky Wesleyan before drifting off to Europe and oblivion.

From 1965 through '78, the state tournament was held every year in Freedom Hall, a 14-year span that included its share of stunning upsets, buzzer-beating shots, and sensational individual performances. Some of the best:

• In the 1965 semifinals, Breckinridge County trailed Hazard by seven with 5:33 to go and star Butch Beard on the bench with four personal fouls. But the Bearcats gathered themselves for a comeback that pulled them within 67-66. After Hazard's Chester Rose made a layup with 1:03 remaining, Breckinridge held the ball until 23 seconds remained, when Jay Harrington was fouled. He made both free throws and the Bearcats added three more for a 72-68 victory. In the title game, Beard scored 30 in a 95-73 blowout of Holy Cross.

• The 1966 state tournament was the first in which Louisville had two regional champions and one of them, Male, made the final against Shelby County and its bow-legged star, Casey. The Rockets jumped out to a 10-point lead in the first quarter and held on for a 62-57 win behind Casey's 23 points, eight rebounds, and six assists.

• In 1967, Allen County came to Louisville with a 32-1 record and Jim McDaniels, the first 7-footer to play in the "Sweet Sixteen," but McDaniels got into foul trouble against Central in the quarterfinals and the Patriots lost, 72-66. That opened the way for dark horse Earlington, a 250-student school in Hopkins County, to win one for the rural schools. With his team trailing Covington Catholic 53-53 with six

The Courier-Journal
Future WKU star Jim McDaniels (44) celebrates an Allen County victory in 1967.

The Courier-Journal
Seneca was no match for Glasgow's press and star Jerry Dunn in the 1968 title game.

seconds remaining, Earlington's Justin Sharp fired up a 35-footer. The shot missed, but the rebound went to Tyrone Hopson, standing flat-footed about 15 feet from the basket.

He knocked in the game winner as time expired. "I didn't really have time to think about missing," Hopson said.

• In the 1968 title game, Glasgow's Jerry Dunn torched Seneca for 33 in the Scotties' 77-68 victory. Dunn and his coach, Jim Richards, both moved on to Western Kentucky, where Dunn was a starter and Richards an assistant on the Hilltoppers' 1971 NCAA Final Four team. The title was a wonderful gift for Glasgow native Louie B. Nunn, Kentucky's first Republican Governor in decades. He let Richards and his wife ride home in his state limousine.

• In 1969, William "Bird" Averitt of Hopkinsville drove for a layup with seven seconds remaining to give his team a 69-67 win over Hazard. Averitt, who later played pro ball with the Kentucky Colonels, scored 11 of his team's last 15 points. That also was the year Central's King torched Ohio County for 44 points in the championship game, breaking Cliff Hagan's record of 41 set in 1949.

• Male became the only school to win back-to-back titles in Freedom Hall, prevailing in both 1970 and 1971 for Coach Jim Huter. The Bulldogs were built around such stars as William Gordon, Bill Bunton, and Larry Harrelson. In the 1971 semifinals, Anderson County blew an 11-point lead against Central and found itself trailing, 62-60, with eight seconds to go. The inbounds pass went to Jimmy Dan Conner, who knocked down the tying field goal and the ensuing free throw to enable Anderson to get the win. In the title game, however, Male prevailed, 83-66, behind Gordon's 29 points.

• In his eighth state tournament as Owensboro's coach, Bobby Watson finally won the title when his Red Devils defeated Elizabethtown, 71-63, in the 1972 title game. Louisville Central made a splash in the opening round, setting a new record for points while routing Paducah Tilghman, 123-87. But the Yellow Jackets got their come-uppance in the quarterfinals, losing to Maysville, 83-70.

• Shawnee injected a healthy dose of soul into the 1973 tournament, beginning with husky James "Honey Bee" Gordon, the Shawnee coach, who had a special gold-and-white striped chair set up for him at the end of the Indians' bench. As he perched there before Shawnee's first-round game against Boyd County, resplendent in a purple jump suit, Gordon was asked if the chair was as comfy as it looked.

"Not bad," he said, twisting a blue towel in his large hands.

At the other end of the floor, Shawnee's cheerleaders did some fancy steps to the soul music generated by the school's pep band high up in the bleachers. Two of the cheerleaders proudly said they were going steady with members of the team.

Shawnee boogied past Boyd County, 85-68, and then denied Male a third straight title, 81-68, in the first-ever title game between two Louisville schools. Ronnie Daniel and Wayne Golden led Shawnee with 33 and 26 points, respectively.

• In 1974, Central Coach Bob Graves won his second title in five years. The Yellow Jackets rolled through the tournament with ridiculous ease – 87-58 over Anderson County in the first round, 95-55 over Taylor County in the quarterfinals, and 92-37 over Greenup County in the semis. In the championship game, they were pushed by Male, making its fourth consecutive title-game appearance, before winning, 59-54, behind Darryl Yarbrough's 22 points.

• Of all the stars who played in State Tournament games in Freedom Hall, none was more ballyhooed than Male's Darrell Griffith, whom college scouts began recruiting in the eighth grade. By the end of his junior season in 1975, which concluded with Male's 76-59 win over Henry Clay in the title game, Griffith was regarded as the nation's top college prospect – even more avidly sought than Unseld in 1964 – and teammate Bobby Turner wasn't far behind.

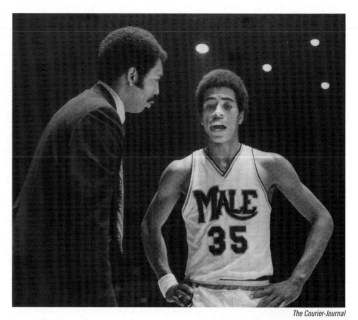

The Courier-Journal

Male coach Wade Houston and star Darrell Griffith.

Only 6-3, Darrell Griffith supposedly had a 44-inch vertical leap. Alas, however, the great expectations proved too much for Griffith, Turner, and their teammates in 1976, when Male was upset by Ballard in the regional and didn't even get the chance to defend its state title. With Male out of the way, dark horse Edmonson County

The Courier-Journal

A Henry Clay fan enjoys a confetti shower.

won the title for Coach Bo Davenport, defeating Christian County, 74-53, in the title game.

• In the 1977 championship game, Ballard's Jeff Lamp scored 44 in a 68-59 win over Valley, tying the title-game scoring record. Lamp went to Virginia, where he starred alongside 7-4 Ralph Sampson on the Cavalier's 1981 NCAA Final Four team.

• In 1978, Apollo High of Owensboro came to Louisville with a 33-0 record, only to get upset by Shelby County, 62-55. Shelby's 6-6 Charles Hurt, who went on to a fine career at UK, made a layup with two minutes remaining to put

Shelby ahead for good. Shelby's Mike George protected the lead down the stretch by making five free throws.

The State Tournament moved to Lexington's 23,500-seat Rupp Arena in 1979 and returned to Freedom Hall only five more times. In 1980, Owensboro won another title for Watson when Chip Watkins of Louisville Doss missed a 15-footer in the final seconds to allow the Red Devils to escape, 57-56.

The "Sweet Sixteen" didn't return to Louisville until 1988, the year – as we shall see -- of an historic title game between Clay County and Ballard. After another year in Rupp Arena, it returned to Freedom Hall in 1990 and was again won by a Louisville school, Fairdale, which defeated Covington Holmes, 77-73, for the title. A year later, Fairdale defeated Tates Creek, 67-63, in Rupp Arena to make it two-in-a-row for Coach Stan Hardin and his star players, Jermaine Brown and Maurice Morris.

Back in Freedom Hall in 1992, the tournament was won by University Heights, a private school in Warren County that defeated another private school, Lexington Catholic, 59-57,

in the championship game. Due partly to the private schools' small followings, total tournament attendance dipped under 100,000 for the first time since 1980.

The last state tournament in Freedom Hall was the 1994 event, and the title went to Fairdale, which defeated Lexington Paul Dunbar, 59-56, in the title game. This time Fairdale was coached by Lloyd "Pink" Gardner, longtime assistant to Stan Hardin. Before that, Gardner had been the team manager for the Kentucky Colonels of the ABA.

Maybe it was the greatest Kentucky state high school championship game ever, and maybe it wasn't, but the 1988 renewal in Freedom Hall certainly had all the state tournament elements that have enchanted generations of Kentuckians. It matched a little team from the mountains (Clay County) against a powerhouse from Louisville (Ballard); two fiery coaches in Clay County's Bobby Keith and Ballard's Scotty Davenport; and, most importantly, two brilliant players in Clay County's Richie Farmer and Ballard's Allan Houston.

At 6-5, Houston had five inches on Farmer in height, and

Chris Hall

Faridale High School stars Rashawn Morris (left), Eric Martin (center), and Terrance Jones (right) helped win two state titles in Freedom Hall.

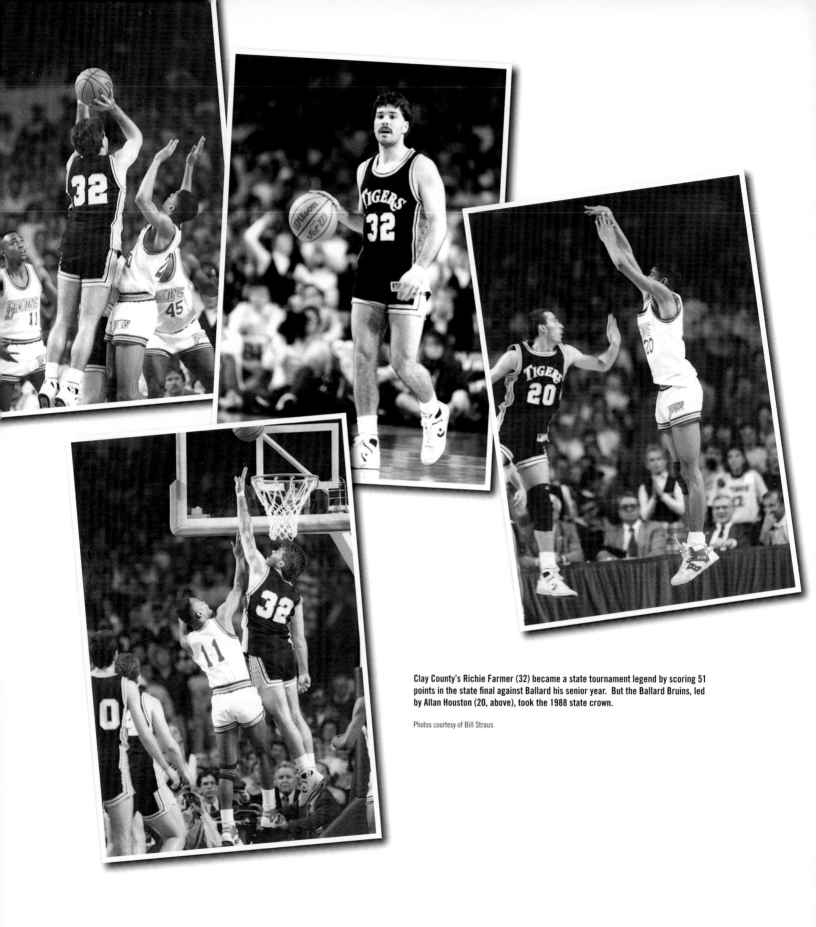

Clay County's Richie Farmer (32) became a state tournament legend by scoring 51 points in the state final against Ballard his senior year. But the Ballard Bruins, led by Allan Houston (20, above), took the 1988 state crown.

Photos courtesy of Bill Straus

at least that much in wingspan, but Farmer, with his bushy mustache and 5 o'clock shadow, looked years older. Both were exceptional outside shooters. But while Houston was bound for the University of Louisville (he later switched to Tennessee when his father Wade accepted the head coaching job there), Farmer was considered by some to be too small or too slow or too something to play for a top Division I college team.

Even before the final game, Farmer was a Kentucky basketball icon. The 1988 state tournament was his fifth in a row. He led Clay County to a runner-up finish as a freshman in 1985 and to the state title as a junior in 1987. But both those tournaments were held in Rupp Arena, where the crowds always rooted as hard for the mountain teams as they pulled against the Louisville schools. His critics felt that Farmer might be out of his comfort zone in Freedom Hall.

Yeah, right.

In the opening round, Farmer introduced himself to Freedom Hall by torching Rowan County for 38 in an 83-52 victory. He added 48 more in wins over LaRue County and Pleasure Ridge Park. Then came the most eagerly-anticipated championship game rematch in tournament history. On the other side of the bracket, Ballard had breezed past Laurel County, Covington Holmes and Apollo.

Only a year after leading Clay County to a 76-73 overtime win over Ballard in Rupp, Farmer electrified a SRO crowd of 19,575. All he did against Ballard's double-teaming pressure was score 51 points, seven more than anybody had ever gotten in a championship game. Nine of his field goals were three-pointers, another record.

But it wasn't enough to prevent Ballard from winning, 88-79. Houston was brilliant with 23 points. But the game belonged to Farmer, who played all 32 minutes despite being worn out from the 92-90 win over PRP that morning. Besides his 51 points, he had six assists, seven rebounds, and only two turnovers.

Farmer's signature move was to back a defender toward the goal, then spin and fire a fall-away jumper that was impossible to block. Sometimes, though, he would simply fire away as soon as he caught the ball. His range was virtually unlimited.

"I think that Richie Farmer is the best guard in America," said Clay County coach Keith. "He dominated the state tournament more than anybody since Wes Unseld in 1963 – and Unseld was a center while Richie's a guard."

As he sat on the Clay County bench, clutching a black towel that he occasionally used to mop his face, a dog-tired Farmer shed no tears, made no excuses, and took no particular pride in his performance-for-the-ages.

"The MVP trophy is nice, but I'd rather have the big trophy," he said. "We've accomplished a lot – took the championship back to the mountains last year for the first time in a while. But we're kinda greedy. We wanted this one, too."

Howard Schatzberg
CH OUR CHARMING LADY, ridden
by Mary Marcum Orr and owned by
Donna and Jack Finch

WORLD'S CHAMPIONSHIP HORSE SHOW

A couple of days before the Five-Gaited Championship Stake at the 1982 Kentucky State Fair World's Championship Horse Show, Don Harris sat in a gray director's chair and talked about the business and Imperator, its reigning star. A gentle breeze stirred the curtains that covered his tack room doors and the branches of the potted plants that made the place seem more like a drawing room than a barn. "This is the one that everybody wants," Harris said, "and right now I feel that Imperator is better than he has ever been in his life."

For Imperator, the show goes on with style, flair

Billy Reed
Courier-Journal sports editor

Imperator scores another victory, winning the five-gaited gelding championship. Story, Page D-3.

Imperator and Don Harris brought rare regional and national attention to the horse show world.
Reprinted with permission from *The Courier-Journal*

At the time, Imperator was a celebrity in the horse show world. He received about 300 fan letters a year, said Harris, and some of his fans came from around the country to visit him at home – the Don Harris stable in Simpsonville. Why, even Muhammad Ali once dropped by to see Imperator when he was competing at Madison Square Garden in New York. Still, said Harris, it bothered him that the stars of the saddlebred world didn't get nearly as much publicity as their counterparts from thoroughbred and harness racing.

"I like to tell people that if they come to a horse show," Harris said, "they can see horses that perform with more style and brilliance than any other breed. That's true of any horse show, but especially the world's championship show. There are a lot of horses who can't win a ribbon in Freedom Hall, but who could go to any other show and win."

A gelding, Imperator had won the previous two world's championships in the five gaited stake that's the marquee event at any saddlebred event. It takes a special horse to execute five different gaits – walk, canter, trot, slow gait and rack – with enough aplomb and style and flair to turn on the crowd and the judges. And there was no doubt that Imperator was a special horse, worthy of inclusion on the list of the sport's all-time great – a list that included names such as Wing Commander, My My, Lady Carrigan, and Yorktown.

Doug Shiflet
CH IMPERATOR, ridden by Don Harris and owned by Finisterre Farm

Doug Shiflet
CH SKYWATCH, ridden and owned by Michele Macfarlane, Scripps Miramar Ranch

Doug Shiflet
CH SULTAN'S STARINA, ridden by Don Harris and owned by Flying V Farm

Doug Shiflet
CH MEMORIES' CITATION, ridden by Mitchell Clark and owned by Ellen Scripps Davis, Michele Macfarlane, Scripps Miramar Ranch

Doug Shiflet
CH REEDANN'S NIGHTY NITE, ridden and owned by Jean McLean Davis, Oak Hill Farm

Doug Shiflet
CH SKYWATCH, ridden by Mitchell Clark
and owned by Michele Macfarlane,
Scripps Miramar Ranch

Shiflet

Doug Shiflet
CH SULTAN'S STARINA, ridden by
Tom Moore and owned by Vanier

IN MEMORIAM

My My

My My, Owned By
Miss Jolie Richardson
Ridden by Frank Bradshaw

Kentucky State Fair
Horse Show

1969 *August 18-23*   *Official Program* $1.00

If Harris was worried about a younger challenger named Sky Watch, he didn't show it. Trained and ridden by Mitchell Clark, a grandson of the legendary Garland Bradshaw, Sky Watch was bigger physically than Imperator. But it remained to be seen if he and Clark had the poise and showmanship to unseat the champion. Talking about Imperator, Harris oozed confidence.

"He has so much pizzazz," he said. "His form just makes him different, that's all. He's got as much publicity as any show horse ever has, I guess, but that's still only half of what he deserves. If he shows like I think he will, he'll bring the house down."

For years, newspaper editors have argued about whether horse shows are sports news or society news. This sort of offends people in the show horse industry. They believe that showing horses requires every bit as much discipline, skill, and poise as, say, diving, gymnastics or other athletic endeavors that are judged instead of measured.

The Kentucky State Fair World's Championship Horse Show is the game's Kentucky Derby, its Super Bowl, its Miss

Bill Munford (second from left) managed the World Championship Horse Show from 1973 through 2001.

America pageant. In 2008, the show attracted more than 2,000 horses from more than 30 states, Canada, England, and South Africa. The horses compete for a total of $1.2 million in prize money in nine divisions – fine harness, saddlebred pleasure, roadster, etc. – but the glamour event is the Five-Gaited World's Grand Championship Stake.

Of all the trainers and riders who have competed for the most coveted title of all, only four – Earl Teater, Frank Bradshaw, Michele Macfarlane, and Merrill Murray – have won it with three different horses. Macfarlane, who trained and rode Sky Watch late in his career, also has many amateur world champion titles to her credit. They are regarded as highly in the American saddlebred world as Bill Shoemaker and D. Wayne Lukas are in thoroughbred racing, or Stanley Dancer and Billy Haughton in standardbred racing.

Although the Kentucky State Fair has been holding horse shows since 1902, it didn't officially get the World's Championship designation until 1917. "It was supposed to go either here or to Missouri," said Scarlett Mattson, the show director since 2001, "but Missouri didn't want it." For which Kentucky owes the "Show-Me State" a big thank-you. Every year the World's Championship Horse Show pumps millions into the Louisville economy.

"People need to know how important the horse show business is," Harris said. "Why, I'll bet the Kentucky State Fair Horse Show will do more for the local economy than the Kentucky Derby. The Derby is a one-day, one-shot deal. But our people come in here and spend a week or ten days. They spend a lot of money, too."

Although it is best known for basketball, Freedom Hall was mainly designed to be the home of the Kentucky State Fair Horse Show and it has served that purpose well from 1956, when Dream Waltz broke up Lady Carrigan's stranglehold on the Five-Gaited World's Grand Championship, until now. After all these years, Freedom Hall still is regarded as the best horse show facility in the nation, if not the world.

Scarlett Mattson's grandmother, Blanche Bandy, brought her to the first World's Championship Horse Show held in Freedom Hall. She still lives in Irvington, site of the family farm, and she began showing horses when she was 14. Although she had attended horse shows at the old fairgrounds, she wasn't prepared for what she experienced the first time she stepped into Freedom Hall.

"It was just so big," she said. "And I remember they put a spotlight on the winners, which we had to stop doing when they got a new lighting system. I remember my grandmother saying, 'They'll never pay off this place.' But I fell in love with the place, and I'm still in love with it after coming to work here almost every day since 1978."

She worked for Bill Munford, the horse show manager, from 1973 until he turned the job over to her in 2001. A feisty sort, Munford got fired in 1975 for raising too much Cain about the chickens and other livestock that were housed in the horse show barns. But he was re-instated by Governor Julian Carroll and stayed to preside over the steady growth of the nation's most important show.

Munford was the man in charge on April 3, 1974, when a killer tornado cut through Louisville and flattened almost all the horse barns. "I'd left there only ten minutes before," Munford said. "It was a mess, but we had everything fixed up in time for the state fair show."

Horse shows don't get as much attention as horse racing because, for one thing, they're harder to understand. All that matters in a horse race is getting to the finish line first. In a

WORLD'S CHAMPIONSHIP
HORSE SHOW
* * * * * * * * * * *
FREEDOM HALL—LOUISVILLE, KY.
September 9-14, 1957

GENERAL ADMISSION

$.90
Monday through Thursday

$1.25
Friday and Saturday nights

$.50
for Children each night

RESERVED SEATS

$2.50
Friday night

$3.00
Saturday night

JAN GARBER
and his world-renowned orchestra

ADDED ATTRACTIONS

Jimmy Richardson at the organ

Victor Adding Machine 6-Pony Hitch
Anheuser-Busch 6-Midget-Mule Hitch

KENTUCKY STATE FAIR
LOUISVILLE

The tornado of April 3, 1974, flattened several barns used at the World's Championship Horse Show.

horse show, it's a matter of convincing the judges that your horse is the prettiest, smartest, and most disciplined one in the ring.

This is a difficult proposition, judges being the perverse and subjective people they are. You never know what a particular judge might like to see in a horse. So all you do is take your best shot and smile bravely and pray that your horse doesn't get spooked by the crowd or forget what you spent all those hours teaching him. Or that some competitor doesn't get away with employing some gamesmanship against you in the ring.

"Yeah, sometimes people will maybe try to play a little game with you," Harris said. "They may try to meet me on the ends of the right or try to pass me on the rack or the trot, the two gaits that have some speed to 'em. Or they play a little chasin' game. I've been at it so long, though, that I'm used to it."

Tom and Donna Moore trained numerous World's Champions in all divisions before their divorce, and competed against each other afterwards. Donna showed actor William Shatner's horses for awhile and once, as legend has it, she rode up alongside her ex-husband and snarled, "C'mon, let's give 'em a show to remember." That was pretty cheeky considering that Tom had trained and ridden Yorktown to three World's Five-Gaited Grand Championships (1970-1972), as well as seven three gaited horses and three fine harness horses to World's Grand Championships in Freedom Hall.

A person doesn't necessarily have to be rich to own show horses, but it helps —especially if you want to compete at the highest level. After all, the prize money is such that an owner generally won't even be able to make expenses. For example, the purse for the World's Five-Gaited Championship is only $100,000, which is peanuts compared to the $4 million

Doug Shiflet

CH YORKTOWN, ridden by Tom Moore and owned by Jean McLean Davis, Oak Hill Farm

Howard Schatzberg

Actor William Shatner (*Star Trek, Boston Legal*) in action at Freedom Hall.

Doug Shiflet

The winning rides were photographed by Harry Leon Sergeant ("Sarge"), left, for over forty years. Doug Shiflet, right, and Howie Schatzberg are now the official photographers.

purse offered for thoroughbred racing's Breeders Cup Classic. Only the well-to-do can afford to compete mostly for ribbons and silver.

The 150 or so trophies awarded to the winners at the Kentucky State Fair World's Championship Horse Show are valued at more than $1 million and kept in a vault in Freedom Hall. The winners don't get to take them home, but they do receive smaller trophies that they can keep. The winner of the World's Five-Gaited Grand Championship is awarded a ribbon, a blanket of roses, and the Oak Hill Farm – Dixiana Perpetual Trophy, a sterling silver punch bowl on a sterling silver base that dates back to the 1920s. It's a half-inch thick and approximately 18 inches in diameter.

Still, it's the love of horses and the pleasure of competing that motivates almost everyone in the horse show world. That's especially true of those owners good enough to compete at the nation's three best horse shows. Of those, two are in Kentucky – the Kentucky State Fair and the Lexington Junior League in Lexington. The other is the American Royal in Kansas City.

Although it's possible for small-time owners to get good horses, the owners of the world champions tend to be people like the owners of Imperator – Curtis Meanor, a federal judge from New York, and his wife, Dr. Geraldine Meanor, a specialist in internal medicine. Ted Turner, the Atlanta-based communications and sports mogul, used to reserve a box at the World's Championship Horse Show. The actor William Shatner, star of the original *Star Trek* series and *Boston Legal*, has campaigned and still shows horses at the highest level.

To the uneducated observer, the horse show scene can be both bewildering and intimidating. An organist, Gene Wright of Shelbyville, provides background music, and announcer Peter Doubleday of South Pines, South Carolina, and Peter Fenton of Pleasureville, Kentucky keep the audience and exhibitors informed. Ringmaster, paddock master, stewards, ring clerks, the office staff and many others make the horse

Even at the highest level, saddlebred horse owners compete more for silver and ribbons than for money. The trophies awarded at the World's Championship Horse Show are valued at more than $1 million.

Avis

There have been many people who, as amateurs, have been prominent exhibitors for many years. One is Jean McLean Davis, owner of Oak Hill Farm in Harrodsburg, Kentucky, who donated the sterling silver base for the Oak Hill Farm – Dixiana Perpetual Trophy (at left), which dates back to the 1920s.

Jean owned the World's Five Gaited Grand Champions, CH Oak Hill's Chief, CH Yorktown and CH Man On The Town. Her three gaited World's Champions are Oak Hill's Dear One, Home Town Hero, and Gimcrack, the only horse she rode herself. She also won many ladies and amateur championships in three gaited, five gaited and fine harness divisions.

Another successful exhibitor is Mary Gaylord McClean, who not only showed but bred According To Lynn, a two-time reserve World's Grand Champion five gaited horse. She has also been successful in the Hackney/Harness pony division, winning many amateur and open World's Championships.

Barbara Goodman Manilow and Carol Hillenbrand are amateurs who have had many World's Champions in amateur and ladies three gaited and five gaited divisions as well.

Lillian and Raymond Shively are a couple who have trained and shown many World's Champions in amateur, junior exhibitor, ladies and open divisions. Lillian has trained numerous equitation champions. Raymond is known for his ability with roadster horses, which are standardbreds, winning the World's Grand Championship fourteen times.

The Courier-Journal *Magazine*
Helen Crabtree was an expert at training championship horses and riders.

billy reed
Courier-Journal Sports Editor

Arm torn by stallion, Crabtree's appearance a triumph of courage

He was putting a blanket on the stallion's back when it happened. The horse suddenly wheeled and sank his teeth into Redd Crabtree's left arm. For a few horrible moments, the 1,500-pound stallion flung the 150-pound man around the stall, as if he were a rag doll. The horse let go only when Redd's father smashed him in the head with a bucket.

His parents, Charlie and Helen, rushed Redd from their Simpsonville, Ky., farm to Suburban Hospital in eastern Jefferson County, where he underwent emergency surgery for three hours. The doctors took out eight inches of nerve. When they were through, Crabtree's hand was a limp mass of flesh. His career as one of America's leading show-horse trainers was in jeopardy.

That was April 10.

Last night Crabtree rode Cora's Time to victory in the five-gaited World Grand Championship at the Kentucky Sate Fair. The horse he beat, defending champion Belle Elegant, not only used to be part of Crabtree's stable, but is a full sister to the stallion (Valley's Desdemona Denmark) that almost tore off his arm. Such are the vagaries of horse-show biz.

Crabtree's appearance here was a tribute to both his ability and his courage. Above all, a horseman needs good hands to communicate with his animal. Crabtree's left hand is only about 30 per cent as useful as it was before the accident, which puts him at a terrible disadvantage. He can't even wear gloves in the ring because they deprive him of what little feeling remains.

Yesterday afternoon Crabtree sat in a hotel restaurant and rolled up the left sleeve of his shirt so a visitor could see the purple U-shaped scar left by the stallion's teeth. He slowly made a fist, then relaxed his fingers and said, ruefully, "He really nailed me good . . . just to be here is something I'm proud of."

The Kentucky State Fair Horse Show is the Kentucky Derby of the saddlebred industry. This week, as always, some 10,000 people came to town with 1,700 horses to compete not so much for the prize money, which is minimal, but for the blue ribbons and the simple pride involved in being associated with a world champion.

The five-gaited horses are the stars of any show. They must master three natural gaits (walk, trot and canter) and two learned ones (slow gait and rack). The appearance of a Belle Elegant or Cora's Time never fails to bring shouts of admiration from the capacity crowd of 18,000 or so that always shows up for grand championship night.

The Crabtrees run one of the biggest and best stables in the business. Charlie Crabtree long has been known for his expertise with harness horses, while Helen is recognized as perhaps the best equitation teacher in the country. And Redd, 42, has developed more than his share of world champions — including

See ARM
Page 16, Col. 1, this section

Reprinted with permssion from
The Courier-Journal

show run smoothly. The riders wear hats and expensive riding habits, and some of the tack rooms at the barns are furnished more lavishly than some folks' living rooms.

In recent years, South Africa has become a hotbed of saddlebred breeding and training. In 1997, Zovoorbij Commander in Chief became the first South African horse to win the World's Five-Gaited Championship. He was trained and ridden by Redd Crabtree, a horseman who

has a special place in the hearts of everyone who loves the State Fair World's Championship Horse Show.

On April 10, 1978, Redd was putting a blanket on a stallion's back when the horse suddenly wheeled and sank his teeth into Crabtree's left arm. For a few horrible moments, the 1,500-pound stallion flung the 150-pound man around as if he were a rag doll. The horse let go only when Redd's father, Charlie, smashed him in the head with a bucket.

The Crabtrees – Charlie, Helen, and their adopted son Redd – were arguably the first family of the show horse world. Together they trained, rode and/or drove an untold number of champions. In addition, Helen became known as one of the finest equitation teachers in the nation.

Now Charlie and Helen rushed Redd from their Simpsonville farm to Suburban Hospital in Eastern Jefferson County, where he underwent emergency surgery for three hours. The doctors took out eight inches of nerve. When they were through, Crabtree's hand was a limp mass of flesh. His career as one of America's leading saddlebred horsemen was in danger.

However, only two months after the stallion Valley's Desdemona Denmark almost tore off his arm, Redd was back in the saddle, wearing a cast. But in the first week of June, tragedy struck again when Summer Melody, a serious candidate for the World's Five-Gaited Championship Stake, died of pleurisy. "We probably lost the best saddle horse the industry has had in a number of years," Redd said. "Losing her was a lot more weakening to me than what happened to my arm."

In July, more misfortune was in store for Crabtree at the Lexington Junior League Horse Show. With his arm in a specially-designed splint, he showed Cora's Time against Belle Elegant, the defending World's Five-Gaited Champion. He did well enough to win the blue ribbon. The judges, however, disagreed. "The crowd was for my mare," said Redd, "but they didn't have a card and a pencil."

On the afternoon of the championship night at the World's Championship Horse Show, Redd sat in a hotel restaurant and rolled up the sleeve of his shirt so a visitor could see the purple U-shaped scar left by the stallion's teeth. He slowly made a fist, then relaxed his fingers and said, ruefully, "He really nailed me good…just to be here is something I'm proud of."

That night in Freedom Hall, everything finally came together for Redd. He upset Belle Elegant, whom he had trained in her formative stages, with Cora's Time, a full sister to the stallion that almost tore off his arm. Such are the vagaries of the horse-show biz. The crowd of more than 16,000 gave Redd the rousing ovation he had earned. The Crabtree spirit had prevailed again.

"If Charlie and I hadn't been there," said Helen, "he could have been killed. We never go to see the stallions with him, but we just happened to be there that night. I guess somebody up there was looking after us."

Feisty and flinty, Helen paved the way for women such as Michelle Macfarlane. She was a tough competitor who often groused that men would only recognize her for her teaching, not her horsewomanship. Near the end of My My's storied career, Helen upset her in Madison Square Garden with Legal Tender.

"It's a man's game," she said, "and most of the time I'm just one of the boys. I'm one of the last to beat My My, but I have to keep quiet about it because all the men will get mad."

As Harris expected, Imperator did, indeed, bring the house down in 1982. But so did Sky Watch, the challenger. It turned out to be the first duel in what became the greatest

My My: Ingredients Of A Champion

My-My is a big, light chestnut mare which looks like the biggest cinch since Franklin D. Roosevelt.

At least, that was the opinion of veteran observers Tuesday night after watching Jolie Richardson's 8-year-old star open defense of her five-gaited grand championship by winning the $500 five-gaited mare stakes at the Junior League Horse Show.

Under the skill of veteran driver Frank Bradshaw, My-My looked worth every bit of the $60,000 paid for her by Miss Richardson during last year's show and showed why she has been world's five-gaited champ the past two years.

What makes My-My a champion? Three main factors, according to Miss Richardson.

"First, she was born to be game. She's got spirit and desire . . . she's a powerhouse. Her motion and pace put you in

mind of a stud. She's also very smart and very brilliant."

Second, according to Miss Richardson, is the skilled training and driving of Frank Bradshaw.

"The trainer makes it look easy," Miss Richardson said. "Frank is one of the finest showmen in the world. He makes it look easy, but it's not that easy."

So skillfully does Bradshaw guide My-My that even a veteran horsewoman like Miss Richardson keeps hands off in competition, which is a third reason for My-My's success.

"I'm not silly like a lot of owners," she said. "I don't intend to ever beg Frank to let me ride, unless he says it's absolutely all right. Don't ever let amateurs fool around with stakes horses or they'll ruin them."

My-My, out of old favorite Easter Parade, is best at trotting

and the rack, according to Miss Richardson. Also included in five-gaited competition is the walk, canter, and slow walk.

Taking the reserve champion's ribbon Tuesday night was Star of the Show, ridden by Earl Teater and owned by Dodge Stables of Lexington. Third was Commander's Countess, owned by Paul E. Master of Beverly Hills, Calif., and ridden by Claude Shiflet.

My-My's victory so far was the highlight of a show which veteran manager J. T. Denton believes will match any past Junior League show in success.

"The exhibitors seem impressed with the horses here and the quality," Denton said, 'and our gate is running the same as last year. We're having awfully good crowds.

"It looks like another of the big ones . . . a top show."

The third evening session gets under way at 7:30 o'clock

tonight with three $500 stakes sharing featured billing.

First is the $500 Five-Gaited, Junior Exhibitor's Stake, which has drawn 18 entries. Among the top ones should be Sensational Princess, ridden by Randi Stuart and owned by Burning Tree Farm, and Stonewall Imperial, ridden and owned by Julianne Schmutz of Louisville.

Second is the $500 Junior Fine Harness Stake, which has drawn 12 young entries. Tops may be Starlike, driven by Tom Moore and owned by Knolland Farms.

Third $500 stake and final class of the evening is the $500 Five-Gaited Gelding Stake. Favored to win "The Replica" Challenge Trophy — donated by Miss Judy Marks of Chicago in honor of the former great gelding — is Main Title, ridden by Teater and owned by Dodge Stables.

First event on tonight's card is the $250 Three-Gaited, Junior Exhibitor's Stake, sponsored by The Lexington Leader. Horse to watch probably will be High Point Stonewall, ridden and owned by Julianne Schmutz.

In other classes Tuesday, Look-A-Here captured the $500 Three-Gaited, Three-Year-Old stake. Ridden by co-owner Martin Mueller, Look-A-Here won $120 and a trophy. Mrs. Jean McLean Davis of Harrodsburg is the other owner.

Radiation, ridden by Moore and owned by Knolland Farms, won the $500 three-gaited stake. Second was A Lovely Sensation, owned by the Grapetree Farm of Canada and ridden by Jimmy Shane.

Burning Tree Farms' Legal Tender captured the amateur five-gaited stallion or gelding class with Randi Stuart in the saddle.

Reprinted with permssion from *Lexington-Herald Leader*

rivalry the horse show world had ever seen. To this day, it has been unsurpassed for its closeness and brilliance.

Before Imperator and Sky Watch hooked up, the five-gaited championship had gone through eras where one horse stood unchallenged as champion. From 1948-1953, it was Earl Teater and Wing Commander. From 1954-1958, it was Garland Bradshaw and Lady Carrigan, whose reign was interrupted only by Dream Waltz and Earl Teater in 1956. And from 1963-1968, it was perhaps the greatest of them all, My My, who was ridden and trained by Garland's brother Frank Bradshaw.

At no point in their careers, however, did My My or Wing Commander or Lady Carrigan ever have a competitor to push and test them like Imperator and Sky Watch pushed and tested each other on that historic night in 1982.

During the workout, the Freedom Hall crowd of more than 16,000 seemed pretty much equally divided. Imperator was smaller and daintier than Sky Watch, whose size advantage was apparent every time they got close to each other. "I went into the night as an Imperator fan," said Mattson, "but about halfway

through I switched to Sky Watch."

She had a good eye. The judges also picked Sky Watch, ending Imperator's reign atop the sport but beginning a rivalry that galvanized horse show fans around the world for the next six years. Indeed, Imperator vs. Sky Watch was the saddlebred equivalent of Alydar vs. Affirmed, a rivalry that inspired heated debates – and perhaps even a few friendly wagers – whenever the international horse show crowd returned to Freedom Hall for the one and only World's Championship show.

Sky Watch successfully defended his championship in both 1983 and 1984, but in 1985 and 1986 Imperator returned to the throne. The 1986 renewal of the rivalry was marred when Sky Watch came up lame during the workout. Rather than risk further injury, Mitchell Clark guided his champion toward the exit gate. When he arrived there, he turned Sky Watch around to face the crowd and tipped his hat. The crowd gave its hero the standing ovation he deserved.

Two years later, with Imperator retired to the Kentucky Horse Park in Lexington, Kentucky, Sky Watch made a triumphant return that was made special by the presence of Michele Macfarlane in the saddle. She had replaced Mitchell Clark and became the first female amateur to win the World's Five-Gaited Grand Championship.

Although Macfarlane later won five-gaited world's championships aboard Memories' Citation (1996) and CCV Casey's Final Countdown (2007), and although she became the only rider to win both the World's Five-Gaited and Three-Gaited titles with the same horse (Memories' Citation), she will always be remembered for returning Sky Watch to his previous glory. It was just too bad that Imperator still wasn't around to test him, one more time.

"Many people think the classes between those two magnificent animals will never be repeated," Mattson said. "Those who saw them are still awestruck with the shows they made."

Doug Shiflet

CCV CASEY'S FINAL COUNTDOWN, ridden by Michele Macfarlane and owned by Michele Macfarlane and SiSi Stables.

THE FINAL FOURS

On Saturday afternoon, March 22, 1969, Freedom Hall was packed with college basketball fans eager to see the NCAA championship game between UCLA, which was going for a record third consecutive title, and Purdue, which seemed to be just the team to deny the inevitable. Each team was built around charismatic All-Americans who were as different as two players possibly could be.

For the Bruins, it was Lew Alcindor, the 7-foot-1 African-American native of New York City who was unstoppable in the paint. For Purdue, it was Rick "The Rocket" Mount, the 6-foot-3, spit-curled blond bomber from rural Indiana who could hit his jumper from the parking lot.

Although UCLA was a decided favorite, the Bruins had looked vulnerable in the semifinals, barely surviving against upstart Drake, 85-82. "I feel like I've had a reprieve," said UCLA Coach John Wooden. On that same night, Mount had drilled North Carolina for 36 in a 92-65 Purdue win. It was the second time in three years that

Carolina coach Dean Smith had watched his team flame out in the NCAA semifinals in Freedom Hall.

So who knew what might happen in the arena that had become the Mecca of college hoops? This would be the sixth time in 12 years that the Final Four had been held in the massive 18,500-seat arena at the Kentucky State Fairgrounds. In the previous Final Fours, Freedom Hall had been the scene of several historic upsets. So why not one more ... maybe the biggest of all? On the morning of the game, two Louisville sports writers predicted a Purdue victory, and they looked rather smart when Mount hit his first two jumpers, lighting up Freedom Hall's new electronic scoreboard.

In Kentucky, where great shooters always have been as much appreciated as fine bourbon, the crowd went bonkers and Alcindor's father, who was playing first trumpet in the Bruin pep band, looked ready to swallow his mouthpiece.

Sports Illustrated
MARCH 31, 1969   50 CENTS
THE MILLION DOLLAR FINISH
UCLA'S HAPPY GIANT LEW ALCINDOR

Before he became Kareem Abdul Jabbar, Lew Alcindor led UCLA to 3 NCAA titles.

When the NCAA held its first basketball championship in 1939, the term "Final Four" had yet to be coined, mainly because the tournament field wasn't spread among four regionals until 1952. There were only two regionals that first year, East and West, and a crowd of 5,500 showed up in Northwestern University's Patten Gymnasium to see Oregon defeat Ohio State, 46-33.

The next three championship games were played in Kansas City's Memorial Auditorium, mainly because it was located in the middle of the nation. But in search of a bigger audience (no crowd in Kansas City topped 10,000) and more media attention, the event was moved to Madison Square Garden, the "Mecca" of college basketball located at the corner of Eighth Avenue and 49th Street in New York City.

For six straight years, from 1943 through 1948, the NCAA title game was held in the Garden. Although it drew crowds ranging from 13,300 to 18,479, the NCAA title game was overshadowed by the National Invitation Tournament, which had been a huge hit among the city's sports fans (and gamblers) since promoter Ned Irish started it in 1933.

In 1946, the Garden beefed up the NCAA championship card by adding a consolation game between the regional runners-up. It was the first time four teams appeared at the same championship site. In addition, that was the first year the NCAA title game was televised. An

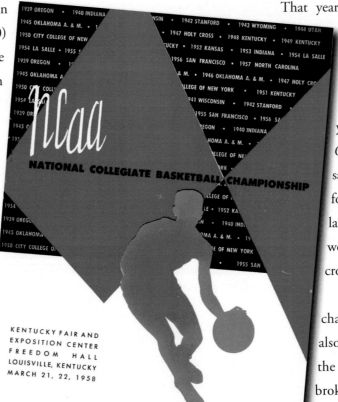

estimated 500,000 tuned in to local station WCBS to see Oklahoma A&M (later Oklahoma State) become the first back-to-back champion, defeating North Carolina 43-40 before a record crowd of 18,479.

After Kentucky won the 1948 championship in the Garden, the NCAA moved the 1949 title game to Edmundson Pavilion in Seattle. Although Kentucky's "Fabulous Five" won its second consecutive title with a 46-36 victory over Oklahoma A&M, the game drew only 10,600, leading the NCAA to return to Madison Square Garden in 1950.

That year City College of New York, coached by Nat Holman, became the first and only team to win both the NCAA and NIT championships in the same year. After defeating Bradley, 69-61, for the NIT title, the same two teams staged a rematch for the NCAA crown ten nights later. This time the home team won, but only by 71-68, before a crowd of 18,142.

But the seventh NCAA championship held in the Garden also proved to be the last, due to the point-shaving scandal that broke in 1952. An investigation spearheaded by Frank Hogan, New York's crusading district attorney, accused 33 players of affecting the outcome of games by "shaving" points in order to beat the published gambling point spread. Some of the accused players came from local teams such as CCNY and Long Island University, but others came from visitors such as Kentucky, Bradley, and Toledo.

All the players admitted their guilt except Kentucky

center Bill Spivey, who passed two lie-detector tests and stood trial for perjury with the jury voting 9-3 in his favor. Nevertheless, Spivey was deprived of his senior year of college eligibility and banned for life from the NBA.

After the scandal broke, the NCAA took its championship game out of New York City and never returned. It held the 1951 event at Williams Arena in Minneapolis, and, bolstered by a crowd of 15,348, spread its 16 teams among four regions for the 1952 tournament. So the first official Final Four was held in Seattle, where regional champions St. John's, Illinois, Kansas, and Santa Clara gathered for the semifinals on Friday, March 25. The survivors, Kansas and St. John's, met the next night, and, before a crowd of 10,700, Kansas rolled to an 80-63 victory behind center Clyde Lovellette.

The event returned to Kansas City's Municipal Auditorium in 1953 and stayed three years before moving to a campus arena, Northwestern's McGaw Hall, for the 1956 event. It returned to Kansas City in 1957 and was rewarded with what still may be the greatest title game ever – unbeaten North Carolina's triple-overtime 54-53 victory over Kansas and its awe-inspiring sophomore, 7-foot-1 Wilt "The Stilt" Chamberlain.

That game captivated the nation's attention unlike any of the previous NCAA title contests and it put college basketball on the brink of a giant leap forward. All the Final Four needed was a venue where it could draw crowds as big as the ones held in Madison Square Garden. As fate would have it, the NCAA's need coincided nicely with the opening of Freedom Hall at the Kentucky State Fairgrounds in the summer of 1956.

Although built mainly for the World's Championship Horse Show, Freedom Hall could easily be converted into a basketball arena seating more than 18,000. When a crowd exceeding that number packed the place for the championship game of the 1957 Kentucky State High School Basketball Tournament, the NCAA noticed and was eager to hear a sales pitch from people like Bill Henry, the first general manager of the Fairgrounds, and Kentucky Athletics director Bernie Shively, who wielded a lot of influence with the NCAA Tournament Committee.

So powerful was Shively, in fact, that he pulled off a remarkable coup for the 1957-'58 season. He was instrumental in getting the Mideast Regional tournament (automatic home of the Southeastern Conference and Big Ten champions) for UK's 11,500-seat Memorial Coliseum in Lexington and the NCAA Final Four for Freedom Hall. This meant that if Coach Adolph Rupp's Wildcat team could win the SEC, which it usually did, it could win the national title without ever leaving the Commonwealth.

As he watched his team get ready for the 1957-'58 season, Rupp was heard to growl: "We've got fiddlers, that's all. They're pretty good fiddlers – be right entertaining at a barn dance. But I'll tell you, you need violinists to play at Carnegie Hall. We don't have any violinists."

This was sad news to Wildcat fans, and not just because it had been six years since Rupp had won the last of his three NCAA titles. The fans were well aware that the 1958 Final

University of Kentucky Audio-Visual Archives
Kentucky's 1958 Champs: The "Fiddlin' Five"

Four was scheduled to be played at the new Carnegie Hall of college hoops – Freedom Hall, just 80 miles from UK's campus.

Unsurprisingly, none of Rupp's fiddlers were named to the pre-season All-America teams that were dominated by Chamberlain, a junior at Kansas; sophomore guard sensations Jerry West of West Virginia and Oscar Robertson of Cincinnati; and guard Guy Rodgers of Temple.

Although the fiddlers hit a lot of sour notes on the way to a 19-6 record – Rupp's worst since 1941 – they managed to win the SEC as usual and earn a berth in the Mideast Regional on their home floor. They whipped Miami of Ohio and its massive center, Wayne Embry, to set up a regional final with Notre Dame. Playing a game that Rupp called "as near perfect as I've seen," the Wildcats held Irish star Tom Hawkins to 15 points and earned their Freedom Hall ticket with an 89-56 win.

In the national semifinals, the Wildcats had a rematch with revenge-minded Temple, a team they had defeated in three overtimes earlier in the season in Lexington. The big play in that game was a 49-foot basket by Kentucky's Vernon Hatton to send the game into its third OT. This time, in a memorable case of déjà vu, Hatton struck again, hitting a reverse layup with 16 seconds remaining to give UK a 61-60 lead. Temple had one last chance to win, only to have guard Bill "Pickles" Kennedy bobble the ball out of bounds, much to the delight of the large majority of a record Final Four crowd of 18,586.

That set up

University of Kentucky Audio-Visual Archives

Coach Rupp admires Johnny Cox's warmup.

a championship game between Kentucky and surprising Seattle, which was led by Elgin Baylor, a 6-5 forward with uncanny body control and satin moves. In the other semifinal, Baylor had slashed his way to 23 points and 22 rebounds in a stunning 73-51 victory over a talented Kansas State team built around 6-9 Jack Parr and 6-8 Bob Boozer. "There's no way we can beat this team," UK assistant Harry Lancaster told Rupp. "Baylor is just too good."

On Saturday afternoon, as Rupp and Lancaster were huddled in a room at the Brown Hotel, forlornly trying to figure out how to stop Baylor, there was a knock on the door. An obscure coach, John Grayson of Idaho State, had come to offer the great Rupp a huge roll of film and advice on how to deal with Baylor. "To beat Seattle," Grayson said, "you must convince your kids that they can't stand there and watch Baylor play … He mesmerizes the other team." He advised Rupp that Baylor tended to foul players who took the ball to the hoop against him. After hearing Grayson out, Rupp told Lancaster to wake up the players 30 minutes early so he could give them a new game plan.

Much to the delight of the crowd of 18,803, another record, the plan worked beautifully. When Seattle coach John Castellani put Baylor on Kentucky forward John Crigler, Rupp ordered the burly senior forward to drive on Baylor every time he got the ball. The result was three quick fouls on the Seattle star, which forced Castellani to put him on low-scoring centers Ed Beck and Don Mills.

To counter, Rupp then ordered Hatton to drive the lane off picks set by Beck, which forced Baylor to either switch off and risk more foul trouble or else let Hatton score easy layups. After the frustrated Baylor picked up his fourth foul trying to block a Mills hook, it was over. Hatton scored 30 and forward Johnny Cox 24 as the Wildcats – violinists, finally – rolled to an 84-72 victory that gave Rupp his fourth title and enabled him to fulfill a vow made when the NCAA hit his 1952-'53 team with the death penalty for recruiting

Coach Adolph Rupp speaks at championship ceremony.

violations: "I won't rest until the man who said we can't play hands me the national championship trophy," Rupp said.

That man, of course, was Walter Byers, the NCAA

executive director. As Rupp gleefully accepted the trophy, he was surrounded by fans, including Kentucky Governor A. B. "Happy" Chandler, the former commissioner of baseball. When Chandler was running for governor in 1955, he called Freedom Hall a "white elephant," mainly because it had been planned under one of his political rivals, Lawrence Wetherby.

The 1958 Final Four was such a huge success that the NCAA brought it back to Freedom Hall a year later. After UK ended the regular season ranked No. 2 in the nation, it looked as if the Wildcats might get to defend their championship in Freedom Hall. However, in the Mideast Regional in Evanston, Illinois, the Wildcats were stunned by arch-rival Louisville, 76-61. When Coach Peck Hickman's Cardinals then defeated Michigan State 88-81 in the regional

Under Coach Peck Hickman, the 1959 Louisville Cardinals upset Kentucky in the semifinals of the Mideast Regional.

The Courier-Journal

How sweet it is: U of L makes the 1959 Final Four in Freedom Hall.

final, they became the first – and still the only – team to play in an NCAA Final Four on its home floor.

Just as the Freedom Hall crowd had been overwhelmingly behind Kentucky in 1958, so did Louisville enjoy a huge home-court advantage in 1959. Unfortunately for the Cardinals, however, they were matched in the semifinals against West Virginia and its great junior guard, Jerry West. Unstoppable on most nights, West ripped Louisville's defense for 38 points in a 94-79 Mountaineer romp. In the other semifinal, unheralded California, coached by Pete Newell, held Cincinnati's Oscar "The Big O" Robertson to 19 points,

16 below his average, in a 64-58 upset.

Newell gave a big assist to Cal's "Straw Hat Band," a group of musicians who came to Louisville in lieu of a pep band.

"They played all over town and gathered a lot of support for us, especially after the hometown Cardinals had lost to West Virginia," Newell said. "So when we had our team meal before the final, I invited the 40 band members to eat with us. Not only did I appreciate their effort, I felt our team needed to relax and enjoy themselves after the furious and emotional experience against the Big O. This was no time for a quiet meal."

On the night of the title game, the "Straw Hat Band" marched into Freedom Hall ten minutes before tipoff, playing "My Old Kentucky Home." As Newell later observed, "That entrance was worth inspirational points. We felt we had inherited the home-court advantage."

The Bears needed every edge they could get. With Cal clinging to a 69-66 lead and less than a minute to go, West Virginia's Bucky Bolyard stole an inbounds pass and passed to West, who got the last two of his 28 points on a goal-tending

The Courier-Journal

West Virginia's Jerry West was Most Outstanding Player in the 1959 Final Four.

call against Cal center Darrall Imhoff. Now leading by a point, Cal pushed the lead back to three when Imhoff put in his own miss with 18 seconds to go. The Bears then kept West Virginia from getting off a shot until 0:03 remained, when they let the Mountaineers have an easy bucket (there was no three-point shot in those days) for a 71-70 victory.

In the consolation game, Robertson smoked Louisville for 39 in a 98-85 Cincinnati victory. "I 'held' West to 38 and Robertson to 39," said Louisville forward John Turner years later. "And you know what? I played good defense."

Returning to Louisville in 1962 after a two-year absence, the Final Four's main storyline was rooted in Ohio. As sophomores in 1960, Jerry Lucas and John Havlicek had led the Buckeyes to the national title in San Francisco's Cow

Palace. They were heavy favorites to repeat the next season in Kansas City's Municipal Auditorium, but were upset in the final by Cincinnati, 70-65 in overtime, the first time two teams from the same state had met for the national title. Ironically, the Bearcats won their first title the year *after* their greatest player, Robertson, had graduated.

Now both Ohio State and Cincinnati were back in the Final Four in Freedom Hall, the Buckeyes facing Wake Forest and the Bearcats playing a UCLA team making its first Final Four appearance for Coach John Wooden. The Buckeyes took care of business in workmanlike fashion, defeating Wake Forest (which was led by All-American Len Chappell and point guard Billy Packer), 84-68. But the Bearcats barely survived against UCLA, winning 72-70 on Tom Thacker's 25-footer with 0:03 remaining. It was fitting that Thacker, a native of Covington, Kentucky, be the hero in Freedom Hall.

So the nation's hoops fans had what most of them wanted – an Ohio State-Cincinnati rematch. Even with Lucas playing on a gimpy knee, Ohio State held its own in the early going. But with the Buckeyes holding a 23-22 lead, Cincinnati went on an 11-2 tear and never looked back. The Bearcats led by eight at halftime and coasted to a 71-59 victory. Cincinnati's massive Paul Hogue outscored Lucas 22-11 and Thacker whipped Havlicek, 21 points to 11.

So much for the previous year's game being a fluke. And so much for the Lucas-Havlicek teams being the "greatest of all-time," as *Sports Illustrated* had predicted after their championship as sophomores in 1960.

In 1963, the Final Four came back to Freedom Hall for the fourth time in six years – and Cincinnati was back, too, trying to become the first team to win three consecutive national titles. The semifinals were laughers, Cincinnati routing Oregon State, 80-46. and Loyola of Chicago routing Duke, 94-75.

Loyola coach Ireland talks to Johnny Egan.

Loyola's Vic Rouse hits the game winner over Cincinnati in the 1963 NCAA final.

While Cincinnati had been ranked No. 1 all season and had lost only once in 26 games, Loyola had emerged from relative obscurity. The Ramblers had only one white starter, Chicago-born guard Johnny Egan, a fact that forced them to deal with such indignities as hate mail and segregated living arrangements in the South. Before a game in New Orleans, they were even threatened with arrest for violating the city's racial policies.

For more than a half, Loyola was no match for Cincinnati, which roared into a 45-30 lead and looked invincible. But then Jucker, fearing that Loyola's 92-points-per-game offense was ready to explode, sent his team into a stall offense (there was no shot clock in those days). Ramblers coach George Ireland countered with a full-court press. "I think they passed up too many good shots when they went into that freeze with ten minutes to go," said Loyola star Jerry Harkness.

They also began coughing up the ball and sending Loyola to the foul line, enabling the Ramblers to pull into a 54-54 tie, when Harkness hit a layup at the buzzer to send the game into overtime. With the score tied at 58, it was Loyola's turn to put the ball in the freezer, which they did until only seconds remained. Unable to get off a shot, Harkness passed to Les "Big Game" Hunter, whose missed shot went directly into the hands of Vic Rouse, who put back the game-winner as time expired. The crowd of 19,193 was a championship game record.

After a three-year absence in which it bounced from Kansas City (again) to Portland, Oregon, to College Park, Maryland, the Final Four made its fifth appearance in Freedom Hall in 1967, at the end of a season that had been dominated by sophomore Lew Alcindor and the UCLA Bruins.

The 7-foot-1 Alcindor seemed quite capable of reaching to Freedom Hall's ceiling.

UCLA star Lew Alcindor tries a "Baby Sky Hook" in his first practice at Freedom Hall.

Photos courtesy of Billy Reed

After winning back-to-back titles in 1964 and '65 with small, quick, pressing teams built around Walt Hazzard, Gail Goodrich, and Keith Erickson, Bruins' Coach John Wooden had pulled off the recruiting coup of all time by convincing Alcindor to leave New York City, where he easily was the nation's No. 1 recruit, and come all the way across country to play his college ball in Los Angeles.

During Alcindor's freshman season, he and his classmates dominated the varsity in scrimmage games (freshmen were ineligible for varsity play in those days), creating a national sense of anticipation unlike any since Wilt "The Stilt" Chamberlain was preparing to enter his sophomore season at Kansas in 1956.

Houston star Elvin Hayes (right) arrives at Louisville's Standiford Field airport.

If anything, the furor surrounding Alcindor was even more intense than what Chamberlain experienced because (a) L.A. was a far bigger media center than Lawrence, Kansas, (b) the college game's popularity had grown enormously, and (c) Wooden had surrounded his 7-foot-1 star with an outstanding supporting cast that included star classmates Lucius Allen, Lynn Shackelford, and Kenny Heitz.

As daunting as advertised, the Bruins arrived in Louisville with a 28-0 record and the burden of great expectations. In their semifinal game, they shrugged off a 25-point, 24-

rebound performance by Houston's Elvin "Big E" Hayes on their way to a 73-58 victory. Afterward, in the locker room, Hayes peevishly told a *Courier-Journal* reporter that Alcindor (19 points, 20 rebounds) was "overrated" and that his Houston teammates had "choked."

After that game, Wooden told his players that he didn't want them to go out on the town because "Louisville is the fifth most sinful city in America." That dire warning puzzled the players, who spent the rest of their time in town wondering what four cities were considered more sinister than Louisville.

In the championship game, the Bruins faced an upstart Dayton team that had shocked Coach Dean Smith's first Final Four team at North Carolina, 76-62. The Flyers, coached by Don Donoher, were led by southpaw forward Don May, who hit 13 consecutive shots on the way to a 34-point performance against the Tar Heels.

As expected, the title game was anticlimactic. The Flyers' single moment of glory came when center Dan Obrovac got the opening tip against Alcindor. Obviously overwhelmed, Dayton missed 16 of its first 18 shots as the Bruins took a 20-4 lead. It got to be 76-47 in the second half before Wooden called off the dogs so the final score, 79-64, was at least respectable.

The next spring, Alcindor was conspicuous by his absence in Freedom Hall. On the way to leading UCLA to a second consecutive title, he announced that he wouldn't try out for the U.S. Olympic team, pleading fatigue. Houston's Hayes and Louisville's Wes Unseld also decided to pass up the Olympics, meaning that U.S. Coach Henry Iba was desperately in need of a center when four teams of college all-stars met in Freedom Hall on March 28 for an Olympic Trials double-header.

Alcindor's long arm stuffs the high-leaping "Big E."
Photo courtesy of *The Courier-Journal*

Alcindor dwarfed the competition in winning three consecutive Most Outstanding Player awards from 1967-1969.

The event was memorable because it was Pete Maravich's only appearance in Freedom Hall. Having just completed his sophomore season at LSU, Maravich was on his way to becoming NCAA Division I's all-time scoring leader. In Louisville, however, the kid who had averaged 43.7 points during the season scored only two, making one of three shots while playing less than half his team's exhibition.

A year later, UCLA returned to Louisville to see if it could be the first team to win three straight titles. In Alcindor's three seasons, UCLA had posted a remarkable 86-2 record. The losses were against Houston, 71-69, in a 1968 made-for-TV extravaganza in the Astrodome, and against Southern Cal, 46-44 in two overtimes, in the final game of the 1968-'69 regular season. Shockingly, the loss to the Trojans came in Pauley Pavilion, where the Bruins had won 52 in a row.

After easily dispatching New Mexico State and Santa Clara in the West Regional, UCLA came out flat against Drake, which forced the Bruins into 22 turnovers and 33 fewer shots. "That's never happened to one of my teams before," Wooden said. Although Alcindor scored 25 points and added 21 rebounds, he sometimes looked disinterested.

Then came the title game against Purdue.

After his making those first two shots, the Rocket lost his sizzle. He missed 14 in a row as the Bruins took control. At halftime, Mount was 3-for-18 from the field and UCLA led, 42-31. Just about everybody in the crowd of 18,669 knew it was over. At the end, it was UCLA 92, Purdue 72. In his final college game, Alcindor had 37 points, 20 rebounds and untold intimidations.

The game was held in the afternoon and UCLA wasn't scheduled to fly back to Los Angeles until the next day, so the players went out for a celebratory dinner at a suburban Louisville restaurant, where Alcindor patiently signed autographs.

"Signing and signing is okay for awhile," he told a *Sports Illustrated* reporter. "But you know something about autographs? You know where they end up? Under the couch, in the desk drawers, stashed away in files and between letters and odd stuff. That bothers me."

Today those autographs are collector's items because, after going to the NBA, Alcindor changed his name to Kareem Abdul-Jabbar.

Mick Jagger, the "Prince of Darkness," performing in Freedom Hall in 1975

CONCERTS FOR ALL MUSICAL TASTES

Blue-gray smoke wisps from the flames of cigarettes whirled and swirled in the eerie translucent green-white-yellow shafts of light that criss-crossed the black cavern of Freedom Hall, and an unholy hurricane of drums and guitars – thunder and lightning – whipped the senses of 18,000 howling souls.

All around the stage, the incredible starship of a stage, the worshipers crowded up close, raising bronze arms in tribute to the devil, standing on chairs and each other, never taking their eyes off The Great Seducer up there mincing, prancing, jumping, twirling, screeching, leering.

This was hell, or, at least, the closest approximation of it likely to be found on earth, and it didn't hurt a bit – thanks mainly to Mick Jagger, the Prince of Darkness, the creator and master of the inferno that is a Rolling Stones concert.

He is either inhuman or super-human, this fiend Jagger. Long brown hair that quickly becomes stringy with sweat. Hollow eyes ringed with mascara, eyes that see everything and see nothing. Oversized mouth from which comes that beautifully awful rasp of a voice. Alabaster skin that gleams in the spotlight when he flings off his coat. An emaciated, neuter body – a body that seems to have neither fat nor muscle nor bone.

But from somewhere, some mysterious source, Jagger generates an energy that is absolutely awesome. Harness Jagger and you solve the world's fuel crisis. For almost two hours, buoyed by the supreme self-confidence that teeters on the edge of conceit, Jagger flung his rag-doll body around the stage – straddling a giant balloon of a phallic symbol, swinging over the masses on a rope, spraying the audience with confetti produced from the mouth of a giant rubber dragon, finally dousing the young Hell's Angels nearest the stage with buckets of water.

He never seemed to tire. Late in the show, when most of the audience was either deaf, dumb, drunk or drugged, Jagger grabbed his microphone and screamed, "You want to rock and roll?" As the roar of affirmation rolled over him, he began to scream "WOOOOOOOOO" and launched into another set of musical acrobatics.

Jagger and the Stones.

In 1964, they exploded out of England at about the same time as the Beatles. Except that while the Beatles were destined to widespread popularity among all ages and classes, the Stones appealed to those of a darker, more revolutionary turn of mind. To many, they were to the Beatles what Elvis was to Pat Boone a generation earlier. They were dangerous, threats to the status quo.

Through the years, the Stones survived changing times and tastes, the drug culture, death, and destruction in their own ranks, not to mention the world at large. Even after a man was stabbed to death in front of the stage in Altamont, California, in 1971, the Stones came back on the strength of Keith Richards' powerful guitar, and, of course, Jagger's inimitable voice and theatrics.

As soon as the word got out that the Stones were adding Freedom Hall to their 1975 American tour, the concert instantly became THE event of the summer. More than 18,000 tickets were sold at Freedom Hall in less than four hours, mostly to products of the 1960s who wanted to see the legendary Jagger while he was still Jagger. The rest of the tickets went to kids who wanted to see legends in the flesh.

The Courier-Journal
Mick Jagger salutes his worshippers in 1975 at Freedom Hall.

The arena went dark about 9:45 p.m. and, when the lights came back on, there were the Stones, with Jagger prancing about in a costume that looked as if it had been left over from the circus (baggy white silk jacket with red and blue stripes, red shoes, etc.). And as soon as the Stones swung into "Honky Tonk Woman," the first few rows of fans, the ushers, and the police disappeared helplessly under a tidal wave of worshippers.

Like lemmings dashing headlong to the sea, the idolaters came in waves, jumping on chairs where there simply was no room to land. When the rightful inhabitants of the seats protested, the kids smiled, shrugged, and offered a joint or a soul handshake. For awhile, it was impossible to move, so all you could do was watch the stage.

If Jagger noticed the disorder, he seemed not to care. In fact, he seemed to revel in it. Once, he looked at a girl sitting on a young man's shoulders and made some come-hither gestures. Non-plussed, the girl replied with some gestures of her own. Sympathy for the devil, indeed.

Musically, the show probably could have been better. Sometimes the songs seemed to run together, one indistinguishable from another. Older fans probably wished the Stones had done more of their stuff from the 1960s. Yet what the Stones did, they did well enough. Besides, at a Stones concert, if you can't get no satisfaction from the music, there's always the spectacle and the bedlam.

At the end, Jagger walked to all points of the starship, sticking his tongue in and out with serpentine quickness. He shook his fist at the audience, jumped up and down, skipped and hopped. Finally, he got down on his knees, put his hands together in a prayerful pose and bowed deeply to the screaming maniacs.

Then the devil vanished, gone in a jumpin'-jack flash, leaving only the smoke and ashes smoldering in the inferno.

The Courier-Journal

The young Jerry Reed was a hit at Freedom Hall.

The Courier-Journal

Lawrence Welk greets his fans at Freedom Hall in 1964.

This was one man's take on an historic concert at Freedom Hall. He's one of untold hundreds of thousands who have enjoyed a musical event in the arena since Pat Boone appeared at the 1957 Kentucky State Fair. Boone, of course, was the anti-Presley, a squeaky-clean guy in white bucks who made a fortune "covering" the songs of black artists such as Fats Domino, who, by the way, appeared at the State Fair in 1958.

Generally speaking, however, rock 'n' roll came slowly to Freedom Hall, mainly because non-controversial, family entertainment was the prevalent booking philosophy throughout the arena's first decade. Some of the better-known stars included Rick Nelson (August 29, 1961), the Kingston Trio (March 18, 1965), The Four Seasons (August 1, 1964), the Lawrence Welk Orchestra (April 1, 1964). Sonny and Cher (November 13, 1965), and Johnny Mathis (August 1, 1963).

But as rock – and its cousin, rhythm and blues – became more mainstream, Freedom Hall began booking some of the hottest acts. On October 1, 1964, Ray Charles and The Beach Boys, representing opposite ends of the cultural and musical spectrums, shared top billing in Freedom Hall, and on May 22, 1965, James Brown, the "Godfather of Soul," made the first of four appearances in Freedom Hall.

Although the Beatles never played Freedom Hall, the so-called "British Revolution" was represented by Paul Revere

Willie Nelson in one of his many appearances at Freedom Hall.

(October 1, 1966), the Dave Clark Five (June 21, 1965), Herman's Hermits (April 21, 1965), and The Monkees (December 28, 1966).

In fact, in the decade from Brown's first Freedom Hall show until the Rolling Stones' 1975 performance, a remarkably diverse array of singers and bands played Freedom Hall: Jim

Bill Woods
John Mellencamp

Morrison and The Doors (October 31, 1968), Ike and Tina Turner (January 30, 1972), Black Sabbath (August 1, 1972), Chicago (November 16, 1971), Mitch Ryder and The Detroit Wheels (February 23, 1968), Sly and the Family Stone (December 12, 1969), Marvin Gaye (September 13, 1974), the Grateful Dead (June 18, 1974), Isaac Hayes (July 10, 1971), Lynyrd Skynyrd (June 24, 1975), the Moody Blues ((November 1, 1973), Three Dog Night (March 24, 1972), and others.

C.D. Kaplan, a Louisville attorney and writer, attended the Janis Joplin concert on June 12, 1970.

"That was way before I started writing as a vocation," Kaplan said, "but it was written up in *Rolling Stone*, as I recall, because it was the first show with the Full Tilt Boogie Band. Her obit said it was among her best performances. She worked to make it work. At one point, the ushers were trying to get people from standing on their chairs."

The pinnacle of Freedom Hall's career as a concert arena came in the summer of 1976. In the four-day period from July 20 through 23, Freedom Hall played host to three of the biggest acts in show-business history – Elton John, the Eagles and Elvis Presley. It was a remarkable tribute not only to Louisville's capacity for pop music, but for the Freedom Hall staff's adaptability and professionalism.

Some of the more fascinating aspects of a big-time concert are the things the public never sees, the action behind the scenes. Months ahead of the show, the staff at Freedom Hall begins lining up ushers, organizing security, making sure the tickets are printed, etc. Their work doesn't stop until long

Elton John (left) and Elvis Presley made the summer of '76 special at Freedom Hall.

after the concert, when the last box-office dollar has been counted and the last long-haired, blue-denimed kid has left the building.

In addition, the Freedom Hall staff must work with the promoters to make sure the stars are treated like kings before and after the show. Most big-time rock stars are prima donnas used to having their every whim pampered. Contracts specifically state what food and beverages are to be stocked in the stars' dressing rooms. If something is missing, temperamental stars have been known to say they won't perform until their demands are met.

During the halcyon four-day period in 1976, Elton John was in the midst of a 16-city, 31-day tour. In Louisville, it took him three days to sell out 20,000 tickets at $8.75 a

pop (steep in those days). Less than 24 hours after John did his third encore and left the Freedom Hall crowd yelling for more, a new stage and sound equipment had been moved in and set up for the Eagles—Don Felder, Glenn Frey, Randy Meisner, Don Henley and Joe Walsh. Some empty seats in the upper reaches of Freedom Hall were proof they hadn't sold it out.

Only two days later came The King, who was beginning a tour that would take him to New England, then down the Atlantic Seaboard. He sold out Freedom Hall in one day, a tribute to the star power he generated until his dying day in 1977. The best part of an Elvis show always was the beginning, when his band would begin to play the theme from "2001: A Space Odyssey." The rustling of anticipation

The King got on his knees to kiss one of his fans during a 1976 concert.

Elvis, at his last Freedom Hall show.

would begin until Elvis burst on stage, nodding and waving as he strode the stage while zillions of flash bulbs lit the darkened room.

At the end of the show, Elvis asked to have the house lights turned up so he could see the crowd. Then he said, "You've been a terrific audience ... if you ever want us back, just let us know and we'll be here."

He was back less than a year later, on May 21, 1977. It was, essentially, the same performance he gave every time he performed – same songs, same souvenir hucksters selling "Super Elvis Treasures," same warm-up acts. But the true-blue Elvis fan didn't care. In fact, Elvis gave them exactly what they wanted. Any deviation would have been unwelcome.

The King was in a good mood that night. Strutting back and forth in his gold-braid-on-white Captain Marvel suit, Elvis smiled (or smirked, it was hard to tell which), then glanced down at a lovely blonde who was standing next to the stage.

The blonde wanted something. No doubt about that. So Elvis, ever cool, obliged. He unwrapped a blue scarf from

The King hits a high note.

around his sweaty neck and flipped it deftly into the blonde's outstretched claws. And he didn't let go. Instead, he slowly pulled the scarf to him as he dropped to one knee.

Then, while 19,000 hearts beat out of control, Elvis leaned over and kissed the blonde squarely on her willing lips. Well, now. Talk about your pandemonium. Instantly the darkened cavern of Freedom Hall was lit by the furious flashing of what seemed like a million Instamatics (this was long before camera cell phones).

As it turned out, that was Elvis' last performance in Freedom Hall. Less than three months later, on August 16, 1977, he died at his home in Memphis of a massive heart attack.

Loretta Lynn: The Queen of Country.

Loretta always looked forward to performing in her native state.

At 2:30 a.m. on Sunday, March 2, 1977, the Kentucky State Fair & Exposition Center was as dark and quiet as a ghost town. The 16,500 people who had attended the Loretta Lynn-Conway Twitty concert had long since gone home. The guards had cleared the parking lot and locked most of the gates.

Behind Freedom Hall, however, the lights still blazed in the $200,000 customized bus that carried Loretta and her entourage around the country. Inside, her driver dozed at the wheel, and Loretta's husband, Mooney, slumped on a seat in a state of semi-consciousness.

But the star, always identified as the "Queen of Country Music," still was going strong. Wearing an orange football jersey with No. 55 on it, Loretta was taping an interview and some promos for a disc jockey from radio station WBKR in Owensboro, Kentucky.

Ordinarily, a star of Loretta's magnitude wouldn't take the time to bother with a small-town DJ, especially after doing a concert and spending another 90 minutes on stage signing hundreds of autographs. But Loretta Lynn, the pride of Butcher Hollow, Kentucky, is different from any other big-time performer in either the country or rock fields. She is uncommonly accessible, cooperative and dedicated to her fans.

So that's why, at 2:30 a.m., long after her crew was asleep, Loretta was doing an interview with "Jake" of WBKR. Not only doing it, but really caring about it. She even got "Jake" to sing along with her on one promo. It was almost as if she were being interviewed by somebody famous, like, oh, Johnny Carson.

"How was that?" Loretta would ask after a promo was done. "That wasn't very good, was it? Here, let's do it again."

And they did it again and again, until both Loretta and the disc jockey were satisfied.

Anytime a star like Loretta does a concert, the demands

are enormous. The fans want autographs, the media wants interviews. Everywhere the star turns, somebody is pulling him or her to do this, tugging at them to do that.

Most stars solve the problem by insulating themselves with layers of bodyguards, agents, managers, and hangers-on. Getting to the President of the United States is probably easier than getting to Mick Jagger or Bob Dylan.

On the way up, it's different. Then the entertainers seek out the public and the press. But once a star is born, the psychology changes. Or, as the manager of country star Emmylou Harris once said when asked if she would do an interview, "Why? She doesn't need it. She's got the No. 1 country album right now."

But Loretta Lynn steadfastly resists the star syndrome, even when she seems on the brink of breaking under the pressure. Touching people and talking with them is the only way she knows how to operate. It's her style, her nature, the quality that has endeared her to millions across the country.

"Well, I like to get down with the people," Loretta said late that night in the dim light of the bus. "If I'm not in no big hurry, I'll sign autographs or pose for pictures as long as the fans want me to. I owe everything to them."

And the press?

"I can usually end up telling more about the interviewers than they can about me," she said. "While they're askin' me questions, I study 'em. In five minutes, I can tell you their life story, what kind of person they are."

Perhaps, because she's a native Kentuckian, Loretta seems to be especially accommodating when she appears in Freedom Hall. Before the Saturday-night show – which, by the way, was the largest indoor audience ever to attend a country-music show in the state – she posed for pictures with officials from the Kentucky Society for the Prevention of Blindness, for whom she is honorary chairperson.

Has she ever had trouble with her eyes?

"I never have worn glasses," Loretta said. "The eye doctor told me three years ago that if I'm a-readin' and the printin's too little, then I'd let my eye muscles get too lazy. It doesn't bother me, unless I'm ridin' on the bus and it's goin' up and down."

After going on stage to do 50 minutes or so of her hits, Loretta sat down with her co-stars to sign autographs. For an hour and a half, she signed pictures, album covers, tape cartridges, scraps of paper, books, copies of her autobiography – anything thrust toward her. One woman even asked her to autograph the soles of her baby's shoes.

"Lord, aren't you thankful you don't have any more that size?" asked Jean Powers of Lexington, president of Loretta's Kentucky fan club.

"I sure am," said Loretta, the mother of six. "Are you kiddin?'"

Somehow, Loretta still seemed fresh and bubbly later in the bus as she discussed the big things coming up in her future. A Loretta Lynn museum was to open in Hurricane Hills, Tennessee, where she now lives, and she was to tape a TV special with Frank Sinatra, of all people.

Also, her new album, "I Remember Patsy," was due out in three weeks. The album is her tribute to Patsy Cline, the country star who did such hits as "I Fall to Pieces" and "Crazy" before her death in a 1962 plane crash.

"She was my best friend in country music," said Loretta. "Patsy was 15 to 20 years ahead of her time. If she was still living, I doubt if anybody would get an award but her. She got the No. 1 girl singer award the year I got the most promising artist award. Patsy told me, 'Loretta, next year you're going to get the No. 1 singer award.' I did, but only because she was gone."

Finally, around 3 a.m., the bus pulled out. Loretta Lynn was on her way to another town, another show, another crowd. She hoped she could catch some sleep on the way.

The young Michael Jackson performs with the Jackson Five at Freedom Hall.

His signature move was the "Moonwalk," in which he appeared to be moving while standing in place. Well, standing isn't quite right. Jackson never stood for more than a moment. He was partial to tight, sequined outfits and made his own fashioned statement by wearing a sequined glove on only one hand.

His snarling, crotch-grabbing onstage persona seemed at odds with the shy, simpering, hand-waving offstage Jackson. He claimed to stand for peace and love, but had a strange way of showing it. All Jackson performances were fueled by a raw level of sexual tension and characterized by suggestive music and lyrics.

Older Americans weren't sure what to make of the androgynous Jackson, which, of course, is one reason why the younger generation loved him. He was a pioneer of the new genre known as the musical video, in which songs would be performed as mini-dramas with plots, sets, and supporting actors/singers/dancers.

The show in Freedom Hall was vintage Jackson, unforgettable for its elaborate staging and pyrotechnics. The crowd roared its approval when he did "Thriller," "Billie Jean," and other mega-hits.

When Michael Jackson appeared in Freedom Hall on April 9, 1971, he was the cute, lovable, early-teen lead singer of The Jackson Five. Backed by his four older brothers, Michael participated in choreographed dance routines, much like the Temptations or the Four Tops or other "doo-wop" groups from 1960s Motown.

But when he returned to Freedom Hall as a solo act on April 20, 1988, much had changed – beginning with his physical appearance. The chubby little kid had morphed into a wraith of a man. His long, black hair framed a face that had been altered and lightened by surgery and other methods.

Only a couple of years before his Louisville appearance, Jackson had become an international superstar and a music revolutionary with his "Thriller" album. Unlike previous pop idols such as Sinatra and Presley, Jackson was as much, if not more, about the dancing as he was the singing.

In March of 2007, when George Strait packed the house in Freedom Hall, the downtown Louisville business community was arguing that the city needed a new downtown arena. However, looking around Freedom Hall, which had served the city and the Commonwealth incredibly well for 50 years, it was difficult to imagine that any new arena could do a much better job of handling a concert crowd of at least 20,000.

Strait performed "in the round," or "in the square" to be more accurate, meaning the stage was set up directly under the big overhead scoreboard. A microphone was set up in the middle of each side of the stage, enabling him to move around and sing to the fans on all four sides.

The sound system was excellent. So were the visuals shown on the large overhead TV screens. No matter where you were sitting — and the place was packed all the way up to the nose-bleed seats — you were able to see and hear Strait as

When Freedom Hall concerts and events are staged "in the round," or "in the square," to be more accurate, performers can move around the stage to be near the audience on all four sides.

well as if you were sitting at home watching a video on the TV in your den. All in all, it was a wonderful concert experience.

Most of the crowd probably came from Okolona, Shively, Pleasure Ridge Park, Valley Station, the counties surrounding Jefferson, and the rural parts of the state.

They were the segment of the population, in other words, that is in the habit of coming to the state fairgrounds for RV and house-trailer shows, livestock shows, tractor pulls, custom-car shows, and gun-and-knife shows. That's probably why there wasn't a lot of hassle involved with pre-concert traffic and parking. The Fairgrounds is like a second home to many of them.

Aside from the performance by Strait and his Ace in the Hole Band, the concert atmosphere in Freedom Hall was excellent. The ushers and concessions personnel were courteous and efficient. The only problem was that the lines at the women's restrooms grew so long that some women began invading the men's rooms. But the length of time that women need for restroom visits is a societal problem that's the same at any public venue, no matter its size or age.

Strait did all his big hits, including "All My Exes Live in Texas" and "They Call Me the Fireman," and you didn't even have to be a fan to be impressed with his professionalism, his work ethic, his politeness, and his interaction with his fans. He didn't talk much during a performance, but he smiled a lot and knocked out one No. 1 hit after another.

He's the strong, silent type who is all about his music. He does a lot of stuff about his native Texas. He's also versatile enough to pull off a tear-jerking ballad or a Johnny Cash rocker with equal aplomb.

All told, it was another memorable night at Freedom Hall. Everybody seemed happy. Even after the new Louisville downtown arena opens, it's quite likely that Freedom Hall will remain the site of choice for a lot of shows, especially from the country field. After all the years, it just feels like home, that's all.

THE KENTUCKY COLONELS AND THE ABA

The American Basketball Association was as close to the circus as a sport will ever get. It bounced to the beat of a red-white-and-blue ball, and it had more than its share of high-wire acts, magicians, animals, freak shows and clowns. But as it evolved from its bush-league opening in 1967 to its final show in 1976, the ABA also came to have a few players and teams of surpassing ability who seriously challenged the established NBA's supremacy.

The league's symbol was Julius "Dr. J" Erving, the gravity-defying, 6-foot-8 wizard who could turn a game into something akin to ballet. He brought elegance and excitement in the same package, making him the league's biggest drawing card. To this day, old-timers love to talk about the first time they saw Erving cradle the ball in his huge hands and do something stunning with it. Every time he played in Freedom Hall against the Kentucky Colonels, the place was packed with fans confident they were going to see something unforgettable.

From beginning to end, the Colonels were one of the league's classiest and most stable franchises. Their first three

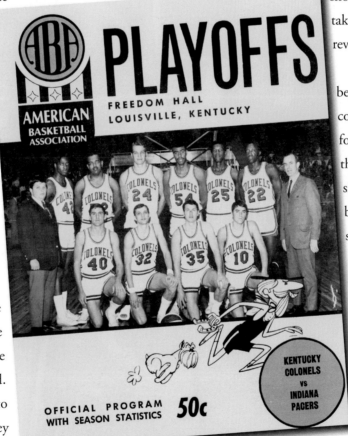

seasons, they played in the old Jefferson County Armory (which had been spiffed up and renamed the Louisville Gardens). Their franchise player was Louie Dampier, the former University of Kentucky All-American whose shooting skills enabled him to take full advantage of the ABA's revolutionary three-point shot.

But the Colonels didn't begin to gain widespread community support until their fourth season, 1970-'71, when they beat out the NBA to sign 6-9 Dan Issel, who had become UK's all-time leading scorer, and moved their home games to Freedom Hall. With the addition of 7-2 Artis Gilmore in 1972, they had the nucleus of the team that, in 1975, won the ABA title to give the Commonwealth its first – and still its only – championship in a major professional league.

It all began on March 6, 1967, when the ABA awarded the Louisville franchise to Don Regan for $30,000. A few months later, Regan sold the franchise to Joe Gregory, Mamie Gregory, and William C. Boone. The Gregorys were wealthy dog show people who installed a prize-winning Brussels Griffon as the team mascot. Nicknamed "Ziggy," the dog flew first-class to

Lloyd Gardner
Julius Erving (32) played in the 1972 ABA All-Star Game in Freedom Hall.

The Courier-Journal
Coming off a pick by 7-2 Artis Gilmore (53), Louie Dampier shows his classic form.

Lloyd Gardner
Dan Issel (44) getting ready to throw one down for the Colonels.

The 1970-'71 Colonels celebrate a playoff victory with Coach Frank Ramsey (right).

owners' meetings and away games, and was assigned a front-row seat at home games in the Louisville Gardens (the old Jefferson County Armory), and treated like royalty in the hospitality room that bore his name.

In any other league, the Gregorys and their dog would have been regarded with a mixture of amusement and dismay. In the ABA, however, they were just another part of the chaotic scene. The league's first commissioner was George Mikan, the bespectacled former All-American from DePaul who had been the NBA's first dominant big man with the Minneapolis Lakers. He did his best to keep board meetings from turning into fistfights, but couldn't prevent a coach from duking out his owner at the league's first All-Star game. Throughout the ABA's history, franchises folded so quickly and often, like cheap tents, that it was difficult to keep track of who was playing where.

The first player to give the ABA a modicum of credibility was Rick Barry, an NBA All-Star who jumped to the new league to play for his father-in-law, Bruce Hale, coach of the Miami Heat. Then Spencer Haywood, hero of the 1968 Olympic Games in Mexico City, opted for the ABA. The bidding wars were terrific for the players and their agents, who played the leagues against each other whenever possible.

Of the players picked by the Colonels in the first ABA draft, the best to sign with the fledgling franchise was Dampier, who had been an All-American for Coach Adolph Rupp at Kentucky. He teamed with former Western Kentucky sharpshooter Darrel Carrier to give the Colonels the best back-court combination in the league. Inside, however, the team had to make due with the likes of Jim "Goose" Ligon, Orb Bowling, and Stew Johnson. They won only five of their first 17 games, leading the owners to fire Coach Johnny Givens and replace him with Gene Rhodes, a successful high school coach at St. Xavier and Male. Nevertheless, their final record was 36-42, tying New Jersey for fourth place in the East Division, and their average home attendance was 3,225.

Lloyd Gardner

Colonels General Manager Mike Storen (legs crossed) has a laugh with his wife Hannah.

Lloyd Gardner

(Left to right) Stuart Jay, Wendell Cherry, David Grissom, David Jones, and John Y. Brown Jr.

In their second season, the Colonels got more national attention from a publicity gimmick – signing female jockey Penny Ann Early to a one-game contract – than from their play, even though they improved to 42-36, made the playoffs (losing to Indiana in the Eastern Division semifinals), and increased their home attendance average to 4,157. After the season, the Gregorys and Boone sold the team to a group of young investors that included Wendell Cherry, Bill DeWitt, J. David Grissom, Stuart Jay, David Jones, Mike Storen, and John Y. Brown Jr. Storen came to the group from the Indianapolis Pacers, where he had been president and general manager.

Under their new ownership, the 1969-'70 Colonels finished with a 45-39 record that put them in the playoffs against the New York Nets, whom they defeated in seven games. But then Storen's former franchise, the Pacers, eliminated them for the second consecutive year.

During the off season, the Colonels pulled off a coup by signing Issel. To properly showcase their new star, they moved from Louisville Gardens to Freedom Hall, where average attendance increased to 7,375 per game. After getting off to a 10-5 start, the team fired Rhodes, replaced him with business manager (and ex-UK All-American) Alex Groza for two games (both victories), and then brought in Frank Ramsey, the former UK and Boston Celtics star who commuted by private plane from his home in Madisonville to Louisville.

Although the 1970-'71 Colonels were only 44-40 in the regular-season, they whipped the Miami Floridians and Virginia Squires in the playoffs to make their first appearance in the championship series. They split the first six games with the Utah Stars before losing the final game on the road. Issel and Virginia's Charlie Scott were named the co-winners of the league's Rookie of the Year award.

After the season, the Colonels and the ABA scored

The Courier-Journal

Dan Issel (44) gave the Colonels an unstoppable inside game.

another coup when Gilmore rejected the NBA to sign a 10-year, $1.5 million contract with the Colonels. (That was huge money in those days). The Colonels also drafted defensive specialist Mike Gale and John Roche, but traded Roche, a New York City product, to the New York Nets. They hired Joe Mullaney to replace Ramsey as the head coach.

Before the 1971-'72 season, the Colonels played three NBA teams in exhibition games in Freedom Hall. On September 22, a crowd of 13,821 watched them defeat the Baltimore Bullets, 111-85, in only the second ABA vs. NBA pre-season exhibition. On October 8, a standing-room only crowd of more than 18,000 saw them take on the Milwaukee Bucks and Kareem Abdul-Jabbar. Although Issel scored 34 points and Gilmore had 18 points to go with 16 rebounds,

Jabbar scored 30 points and 20 rebounds in the Bucks' 99-93 win. A night later, a crowd of 12,238 saw the Colonels lose to the New York Knicks, 112-100.

On January 29, 1972, the American Basketball Association staged the only professional all-star game held in Freedom Hall. It was the second time the game was held in Louisville, and the crowd of 15,738 tripled the 5,407 who attended the 1969 event in the downtown convention center and approached the 16,364 that had attended the first NBA-ABA All-Star the previous year in Houston's Astrodome.

Much to the delight of the crowd, the Eastern Conference team, which included Dan Issel, Artis Gilmore, and Louie Dampier of the host Kentucky Colonels, rolled to a 142-

Lloyd Gardner

Rick Barry (getting the tip) bolted from the NBA to give the ABA credibility.

Still, the Most Valuable Player award went to Kentucky's Issel, who had 21 points, nine rebounds and five assists in a typically solid performance. Gilmore added 14 points and 10 rebounds, but Dampier managed only two points in nine minutes.

The Eastern starters were Gilmore, Rick Barry of the New York Nets, Julius Erving and Charlie Scott of the Virginia Squires, and Issel. The Western starters were Willie Wise and Zelmo Beatty of the Utah Stars, Daniels and Roger Brown of the Pacers, and Donnie Freeman of the Dallas Chaparrals.

A couple of weeks after the All-Star game, McDaniels jumped to Seattle of the NBA. He had reportedly signed a six-year, $3 million deal with Carolina – huge money in those days – but it was what writer Terry Pluto called "a classic ABA play-now-and-get-paid-later deal." In truth, McDaniels got a $50,000 signing bonus and $1.375 million to be paid over 25 years.

"It didn't take long for McDaniels to become dissatisfied with his contract," said former teammate Gene Littles. "He started trying to find a way out of the deal. He didn't play hard most of the time and he was truly an awful defensive player. All he really wanted to do was take that turn-around jumper."

After his All-Star performance, McDaniels got hooked up with agent Al Ross, who had helped both Spencer Haywood and John Brisker jump from the ABA to Seattle. Soon after McDaniels didn't show up for a February 10 game against the Colonels in Freedom Hall, he signed a five-year, $1.5 million deal with Seattle, which also agreed to pay Carolina $400,000 to let McDaniels out of his contract.

115 victory. Also, the East team was led by Carolina's 7-1 Jim McDaniels, formerly of Western Kentucky, who had 24 points and 11 rebounds, both highs for the game.

Lloyd Gardner

In 1972, the Colonels invited Playboy Bunnies to challenge local media personalities at halftime.

The game completed a nice Freedom Hall trifecta for McDaniels. As a high school All-Star, he scored 41 against Indiana. As a collegian, he torched Jacksonville and Gilmore for 29 in a ballyhooed college showdown which Western won. And as a pro, he had one of his greatest performances while playing only 20 minutes.

Secure in the knowledge they were competitive with the best in the NBA, the 1971-'72 Colonels rolled to a 68-16 record and averaged 8,811 at home. Gilmore, who made almost 60 per cent of his field goal attempts and averaged

Lloyd Gardner
The show wasn't limited to the court in the ABA.

17.8 rebounds, was voted both the Rookie of the Year and the Most Valuable Player. But then, shockingly, the Colonels lost their first playoff series to the Nets, who were led by Roche, the dead-eye shooter and slick ball-handler the Colonels had traded before the season.

Before the 1972-'73 season, the Colonels played five exhibition games against NBA teams, three of them in Freedom Hall. The most noteworthy came on October 1, when Abdul-Jabbar and Oscar Robertson each scored 20 to lead the Milwaukee Bucks to a 131-100 victory. The team's newcomers included Rick Mount, the former Purdue All-American who had played against UCLA in the 1969 NCAA title game in Freedom Hall, and Wendell Ladner, a L'il Abner look-alike from Southern Mississippi. Ladner proved to be such a big hit with female fans that he stole a page from actor Burt Reynolds and posed nude for a poster, an ABA ball covering his, ah, private parts.

In his signature moment with the Colonels, Ladner careened into the home-team bench in pursuit of a loose ball, shattering a glass water-cooler and opening a gash in his arms that required several stitches to close. It was typical Ladner, who was known for his brawn but never his brain. Once, when the team was flying into Washington, D.C., Ladner saw the Washington Monument and asked general manager David Vance what it was. When Vance told him it was *The Washington Post*, Ladner only nodded.

Although the team had another outstanding season, finishing with a 56-28 record, average home attendance dipped to 7,113, still one of the best numbers in the

Lloyd Gardner
Wendell Ladner, after plowing into a glass water cooler.

Lloyd Gardner
Van Vance of WHAS radio had a ball as the "Voice of the Colonels."

Colonels' owner John Y. Brown Jr. named his wife, Ellie, to head the team's revolutionary all-female board of directors.

league. Determined to atone for their early flame-out of the previous season, the Colonels defeated Virginia and Carolina in the playoffs to earn the franchise's second trip to the championship series. Once again, however, they lost to the Pacers, this time in seven games. To add insult to injury, the seventh and deciding game was played before a full house in Freedom Hall. This is what *Sports Illustrated* said about the final game:

"The first half of the one-game series was low on scoring and style, and heavy on hand-in-the-gut, elbow-in-the-ribs defense. But then a strange thing happened. In the third quarter, Kentucky's shots wouldn't drop and Indiana was there to get every rebound and stick it in the other end. Kentucky hit only three of 22 for the period and scored but 11 points, an ABA playoff low for one quarter. Given that sort of chance, the Pacers, with (George) McGinnis whirling and muscling for 11 points in a game-turning stretch in which

they outscored Kentucky 14-1, blew out to a 66-52 lead. As McGinnis bluntly put it, 'They just quit. They gave up.'" McGinnis finished with 27 in the Pacers' 88-81 victory.

After that season, when a Cincinnati group expressed interest in the franchise, John Y. Brown Jr., who had made a fortune by franchising Kentucky Fried Chicken, bought out his partners and established his wife, Ellie, as the chairman of an all-female board of directors. If that seemed like a gimmick initially, it turned out to be a masterpiece of marketing. With Mrs. Brown and her colleagues pushing season tickets all over the county, the Colonels' average home attendance jumped to 8,201. Brown also shook up the front office, replacing Mullaney with Babe McCarthy and Storen with Gene Rhodes, the former coach. He also added Adolph Rupp, the legendary UK coach, as vice-president of the board.

Here's an excerpt from the October 7, 1973, *Courier-*

Ellie Brown being interviewed by Heywood Hale Broun of CBS (in checkered coat).

Colonels' play-by-play announcer Van Vance interviews board chair, Ellie Brown.

Journal Sunday magazine article that had Ellie Brown on the cover with Gilmore and Issel in the background:

"Her secret, if she has one, doesn't have much to do with her sex, wealth, or status. Rather, it involves the natural things – warmth, enthusiasm, laughter. In her 33 years, Ellie Brown has learned what makes the world tick, and her background of modest means and hard work enables her to communicate with ordinary working people as easily as she chats with wealthy socialites.

"In her interviews, she prefers to play down her image of 'yachts and limousines,' as she puts it, and talk instead about how she grew up on a farm. About hitching rides into Central City just so she could be a cheerleader. About helping John sell encyclopedias and, later, waiting on tables while her husband made his first million. Even now she says she's not a women's libber, but more of an everyday housewife who just got the chance to do something interesting and fun, who will be glad when all the current excitement dies away so she can spend more time at home with her three children…

"Another nice thing about Ellie is that she's got a sense of humor, even about her husband and his relationship to the team. Before the Colonels hired a head coach, Ellie was likely to say, 'Oh, I think we've got enough coaches, don't you? There's Bud Olsen and Gene and Adolph –- and John.' On another occasion, she was asked what would happen if an interviewer ever introduced John as 'Ellie's husband.' Said Ellie, 'Well, I guess that would be the end of my career.'"

Maybe all this hoopla inspired the team, and maybe it didn't, but the 1973-'74 Colonels posted a 53-31 record and advanced to the second round of the playoffs before getting swept by the Nets. Although McCarthy had been voted co-

Lloyd Gardner

The 1975-'76 Colonels were the last team in franchise history.

Coach of the Year with former coach Mullaney (now with Utah), he was fired after the season and replaced by Hubie Brown (no relation to John Y. or Ellie).

Lloyd Gardner

Neither Hubie Brown's clothes nor voice were subdued.

The new coach loved his nucleus of Gilmore, Issel and Dampier. Both Gilmore and Issel were masters of the pump fake that either led to easy baskets or free throws. And Dampier, by this time, had emerged as the best outside shooter in the league. Although the Colonels brought in a number of guards who were supposed to beat him out – including the heralded Rick Mount – Dampier was impossible to supplant.

The Dampier jump shot was a thing of beauty, an athletic Picasso. The form and style were textbook-perfect, the arms and elbows positioned just perfectly, the ball released at just the right moment. Rupp once called him the greatest shooter he ever coached. And in the ABA, Dampier and the three-point shot were a match made in hoops heaven.

"Louie has exceptional wrist action," said Bud Olsen, a former Colonels player and assistant coach in a 1974 interview. "He releases the ball so quickly, quicker than anybody in the league."

One evening, Dampier showed up at a clinic the Colonels were having for women fans at Durrett High School. His job was to demonstrate the execution of the

The C-J Sunday *Magazine* made Dampier a cover boy.

jump shot. Standing about 20 feet away from the basket, Dampier hit shot after shot. *Swish, swish, swish.* Monotonously, the ball zipped through the nets until, clowning, Dampier threw up a shot that fell a couple of yards short.

"Amazing," said Vance, the Colonels' GM. "He just stood out there and did it like it was nothing, like he was shooting layups or something."

By now the ABA was giving the NBA fits because it had landed some of the most exciting players the game had ever seen. Besides Erving, who began with the Virginia Squires before going to the New York Nets, the list of stars included George McGinnis, George Gervin, Larry Kenon, Moses Malone, Marvin Barnes, and Zelmo Beatty.

Heading into the 1974-'75 season, the Colonels defeated three NBA teams – the Washington Bullets, Detroit Pistons, and Chicago Bulls – in Freedom Hall. That set the tone for a marvelous season in which the Colonels averaged 8,727 in Freedom Hall and posted a 58-26 record to tie New York for the championship of the Eastern Division. After defeating the Nets, 108-99, in a one-game playoff in Freedom Hall, the Colonels then ripped through the Memphis Sounds and the St. Louis Spirits, winning each series in five games, to once again face their nemesis, the Pacers, in the title series.

This time the Colonels were not to be denied. Here's how *Sports Illustrated* reported it after the fifth and final game:

"Kentucky, en route to its first league title, was sidetracked by Indiana only in the fourth game when the Pacers defeated the Colonels, 94-86, at Indianapolis. Pacer George McGinnis broke out of his shooting slump with a 22-point, 21-rebound performance and teammate Billy Keller provided the clutch baskets. The comeback was short-lived, however, as the Colonels withstood a 40-point effort by Billy Knight to take the fifth game in Louisville and wrap up the series, 4-1…The Colonels thus ended seven years of frustration during which they won more regular-season games than any other club but nary a championship."

In the decisive game, Gilmore scored 28 points and grabbed a playoff record 31 rebounds to lead Kentucky to a 110-105 victory before 16,222 fans in Freedom Hall. After the game, Colonels' owner John Y. Brown Jr. challenged the NBA champion Golden State Warriors to a playoff game to determine the champion of all professional basketball. "The public wants it and television would buy it," Brown said. "I think we're better. Remember, I'm a guy who bet on Baltimore and gave 17 points when they played the Jets in the Super Bowl."

The Warriors declined because their league had much to lose and little to gain. Besides, there was a distinct possibility that they couldn't have beaten the Colonels. During the exhibition games, Gilmore had proven he could hold his own with Jabbar or any other big man in the NBA, and Dampier

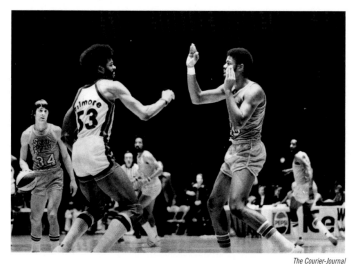

Artis Gilmore and future teammate Maurice Lucas doing Muhammad Ali impersonations.

shot the ball from outside as well as any NBA guard. And Issel had the rare knack of being able to score from both inside and out, enabling him to take big defenders to the perimeter and small defenders into the paint.

The euphoria over the championship dissipated when John Y. Brown Jr. dealt Issel to the new Baltimore Claws franchise (it folded during the exhibition season for financial reasons). Other than Dampier, no Colonels player was more popular than Issel, who sacrificed some of his scoring to accommodate Gilmore. Before the season, the two defending champions – Kentucky and Golden State – met in an exhibition game in Freedom Hall. Although the Colonels won, 93-90, it wasn't the same without Issel.

After Issel went to Denver, he and former teammate
Artis Gilmore battled for position—and victories.

Shortly after the season began, the San Diego franchise folded and the Colonels acquired Caldwell Jones to replace Issel. However, he lasted only a half-season before being traded to St. Louis for young power forward Maurice Lucas. Still, the Colonels' record dropped to 46-38 and average home attendance fell to 6,935.

In the playoffs, the Colonels defeated the Pacers, two games to one, to advance to the semifinals against the Denver Nuggets, who had acquired Issel after the Claws folded. The teams split six games before the Nuggets prevailed, 133-110, on April 28, 1976, in Denver. That proved to be the Colonels' final game.

After the season, the NBA agreed to take four ABA teams – Indiana, San Antonio, New Jersey, and Denver – in a merger that ended the ABA. The Colonels weren't included because John Y. Brown Jr. was unsuccessful in his attempt to recruit partners from the Louisville business community. So, on July 17, 1976, Brown agreed to fold the Colonels for $3 million, which he then used to purchase the NBA's Buffalo Braves.

The big winners were the owners of the St. Louis Spirits, who received $2.2 million cash along with a 1/7 share of each of the surviving ABA teams' television income in perpetuity. Over the years, the deal has put an estimated $250 million into their pockets.

The Colonels' players were put into a dispersal draft. Gilmore went to the Chicago Bulls for $1.1 million, Lucas to the Portland Trail Blazers for $300,000, William "Bird" Averitt to the Braves for $125,000, Wil Jones to the Pacers for $50,000, Jan van Breda Kolff to the Nets for $60,000, and Dampier to the Spurs for $20,000. Dampier proved to be a huge bargain, playing so well in San Antonio that he became almost as popular as he had been in Louisville.

Hubie Brown went on to coach several NBA teams before finding his niche as a pro basketball TV commentator. Over the years, he remained friends with Lloyd "Pink" Gardner,

Lloyd Gardner

Hubie Brown coached the only major professional championship team in Kentucky history.

Lloyd Gardner

Lloyd "Pink" Gardner was the Colonels' trainer before going to a fine coaching career at Fairdale High School.

the Colonels' manager, and his former players. He returned to Louisville for the championship team's 25th reunion in 2000. A few years later, the '75 Colonels became the first team in any sport, at any level, to be inducted en masse into the Kentucky Athletic Hall of Fame.

Although Freedom Hall was the scene of various NBA exhibitions after the Colonels folded, no NBA team ever moved to Louisville. In his autobiography, Issel wrote, "Sometimes I have wondered why it couldn't have worked, why the Colonels couldn't have survived – especially since the people of Kentucky are so crazy about basketball. Reflecting on it now, I can see that there was never a big enough ticket base. And college basketball still is king in these hills."

THE TOUGHEST TICKET IN SPORTS

The Championship Tractor Pull, held each February as part of the National Farm Machinery Show, turns Freedom Hall into an inferno of noise and fumes. It's one of the few sporting events where ear plugs are for sale at the concessions stands. Compared with the tractor pull, a Rolling Stones concert is a night in the library. Nevertheless, each of the five sessions annually draws sold-out crowds of 17,000 or more. A reporter once asked a professional ticket scalper, a man who works all the major national sporting events, which event was the most lucrative for him. "Easy," he said. "The tractor pull in Freedom Hall. Those farmers will pay anything for good tickets."

It's important to know, right off the bat, that the tractors and trucks that compete in Louisville bear only scant resemblance to the ones you see on the roads, fields, and pastures of rural America. You know how NASCAR and drag-racing folks turn ordinary commercial autos into hot racing machines? Well, it's the same with the tractor pull. The competitors take the basic framework of ordinary tractors and trucks, and turn them into huge, gleaming, fantastic machines that belch smoke and fire as they pull their loads down a long dirt track on the floor in Freedom Hall.

A tractor pull is a quintessentially American event. It enjoys its greatest popularity in the heartland. Its heroes are farmers. And it's another manifestation of the nation's obsession with machinery, horsepower, and competition. Every time a tractor churns up the dirt track, the crowd gets to its feet and whoops and hollers.

Some of the spectators are fans of commercial brands. Whenever one of their favorite brands makes a good pull,

A happy ending to a long haul.

they jump up and wave their colored hats – green for John Deere, orange for Allis-Chalmers, etc. Other fans, however, root for certain drivers or representatives from a particular town or state.

"It's unreal," said a fan from Illinois. "The main reason for our growth is that in the winter it's the only motorized sport that you can see indoors. We've got speed on the starting end and power on the finishing end. It's perfect."

Every driver's objective is to pull a weighted sled the farthest distance down the track. (The individual weight classes indicate the weight of the vehicle, not the weight being pulled.) While the driver pulls his or her sled down the track, a weight on the back of the sled moves forward, pushing the nose of the sled deeper into the dirt, making it increasingly difficult for the tractor or truck to advance.

Pulling the weight the full length of the track is known as a "full pull." In 2008, for example, Dennis Boersen of Zeeland, Michigan, won the grand championship of the

Former Kentucky Agriculture Commissioner Alben Barkley poses with a young winner at the National Championship Tractor Pull.

biggest division of all – 10,200-pound Pro Stock Tractors – with a full pull of 248 feet, eight inches. His tractor, named Greenline Express II, is a huge green machine with little tires on the front and giant tires on the back and a big exhaust pipe coming out of the engine and curving over the protective cage where Boersen, wearing a helmet and fire suit, sits behind the wheel.

One of the event's veterans, Esdon Lehn of Dayton, Minnesota, began competing in Freedom Hall in 1977. His tractor, "Red Line Fever," won the 8,200-pound super-stock division back-to-back in 2007 and 2008. He supports his hobby with the money he and his brother earn from a cash-

crop farm. As he looks back over his career, Lehn has noticed an evolution in track-pull drivers.

"The younger kids are more diverse," he said. "They grew up around the sport and went to pulls as kids. Pulls are just one part of their lives."

A case in point was Audra Stratton, who grew up on a farm near Franklin, Kentucky, and was a junior nursing school student at Belmont College in Nashville when she competed in the 2009 Championship Tractor Pull. She started racing antique tractors when she was 13, and moved up to the "big show" as a high school senior. In 2009, she competed in the 9,300-pound Super Farm Tractor division

A 1981 competitor revs up before pulling the sled down the Freedom Hall track.

with a John Deere machine she called "Deerelirious."

"My entire summer breaks are devoted to tractor pulling each year," she said. "But when I'm at an event, I'm working on homework and writing papers in the time between rides."

No wonder ear plugs are popular items at the Tractor Pull concession stands.

Begun in 1967, the tractor pull in Freedom Hall was the first major indoor event and is still one of the biggest. After an

early dispute with the National Tractor Pulling Association, then the largest sanctioning body in the sport, a group of Kentuckians – Billy Joe Miles of Owensboro, Jerry Baird and Carl Mercer of Utica, Donnie Bittel of Owensboro, Joe England of Madisonville, and Walter Harder of Whiteville – decided to pull, run the event themselves, and call it the Championship Tractor Pull.

In 1969, the first CTP attracted 66 tractors in three classes. A year later, the event expanded to two days and added an event. Radio and TV personality Jack Crowner became the event announcer and held the job until 1986, when he turned it over to Lloyd Douglas, a competitor in the first CTP. Today the job belongs to Butch Krieger.

The first truck classes were added in 1977, which also was the first year the event, now spread over four days, completely sold out. A Saturday matinee was added in 1980 to offer 4-H and FFA members a better opportunity to attend a pull.

Over the years, technology has improved the event. In the early 1980s, Jerry Baird developed a measurement system using laser beams and a computer program to accurately

The front wheels of the "Renegade" leave the ground due to the weight on the sled.

record the distances pulled. Drivers now are required to use seat belts, racing helmets, and fireproof suits. As part of Freedom Hall's 1984 renovation, ventilation was improved and a concrete barrier replaced the chain-link fence that

Not your granddaddy's farm tractor.

separated the floor from the first row of spectators.

Thanks to Syngenta, the name sponsor in 2010, and its predecessors, prize money has increased from $5,700 in 1969 to $209,700 in 2009. Nevertheless, even the grand-championship drivers can't win enough money to break even on their investment in their hobby. Some replace normal engines with helicopter or airplane engines. All the pullers buy their own tractors, fix them up, and pay their own travel expenses.

The event has become such a social phenomenon that its fan base has expanded to include city slickers such as Owen and Carol Funk of Louisville, who go each year because they love the crowds, the action, and the enthusiasm. "Sure, it gets really loud," said Funk, "but after awhile you get used to it. It's really a lot of fun."

The program even includes a "Puller's Glossary" for newcomers. Some of the more interesting terms:

Bitin' track – Power track.

Boost – Air pressure generated by turbos or superchargers.

Drop the hammer – Hitting the throttle hard.

Hole shot – Getting the jump off the line, an excellent start.

Hook – Tires getting a bite of the track.

Kill switch – A required hookup that automatically kills the engine if the tractor becomes unhooked from the sled.

Modified – Tractor using any combination of engines, transmission, and final drive.

Pits – Area for pulling tractors and trucks to park.

Pull off – A second run with a heavier sled for the two or more vehicles that make full pulls in a division.

Rat motor – A big cubic-inch Chevy engine.

Transfer – Weight transfer machine to which the tractor hooks to pull.

Wheelie – Lifting the front wheels a desired amount.

In 1993, the CTP's competitive format was restructured to establish a finals round on the last evening of the pull. The winners in each event were recognized as grand champions and automatically added to the event's Hall of Fame. Only the best – or the luckiest – repeat as a CTP grand champion, and only Joe Eder of North Collins, New York, has been a champion three consecutive years. He prevailed in 7,500-pound Modified Tractors in 2002, 2003, and 2004.

A look through the hometowns of the grand champions provides a good feel for the event's national popularity. The champions have come from such communities as Edgerton, Wisconsin; Eighty Four, Pennsylvania; Columbia, Tennessee; Cedar Bluffs, Nebraska; Olean, New York; Athens, Alabama; Melita, Manitoba, Canada; Rhome, Texas; and Lapeer, Michigan.

In 2003, Lisa Tatum of Cookeville, Tennessee, became the first woman to win a national grand championship, taking the 6,200-pound, two-wheel drive Modified Truck

The machines are science fiction made real.

Lighting it up in Freedom Hall.

Division. She made her Freedom Hall debut at 16. While she's on the road as a sales representative for Averitt Express, her parents and other relatives work on her machines. They also keep stats and work the pits at pulls.

"I love traveling, riding motorcycles and horses, anything that can be deemed as daredevilism," Tatum says. "But nothing beats tractor-pulling. I believe that anyone in tractor-pulling has an adrenaline-junkie side to them." Not to mention an amazing tolerance for fumes and noise. At one event in the 1970s, the blue-gray smoke was so dense that a reporter couldn't see announcer John Tong, who was sitting next to him. It has gotten much better since then, of course. Still, it's safe to say that the National Championship Tractor Pull engages the senses unlike any other event ever held in Freedom Hall.

Owensboro native Rex Chapman was a shooting star for the Wildcats.

UK'S HOME AWAY FROM HOME

When Richard "Digger" Phelps became the Notre Dame basketball coach in 1971, he inherited a contract that, at the time, probably seemed like a good deal. Every year, between Christmas and New Year's, the Irish were to travel to Louisville to meet Kentucky in Freedom Hall, then the most famous hoops arena in the land.

The Courier-Journal

"Sit down, Digger, sit down!"

His predecessor, Johnny Dee, loved the series. He liked to call it the "Rose Bowl of college basketball," and never mind

that Dee also went ballistic once when he saw that the game ball was stamped with the autograph of UK Coach Adolph Rupp. For the record, Dee's record against Rupp in Freedom Hall was 2-9.

If Phelps was open-minded when he strolled into the series, it didn't take him long to figure out that playing UK every holiday season in Freedom Hall wasn't exactly

The Courier-Journal

Johnny Dee didn't want to use a ball with Rupp's autograph on it.

in the best interests of either his pride or his team's record. Yeah, sure, the Irish always went back to South Bend with a nice paycheck. But sometimes the money didn't seem reward enough for the humiliation that was inflicted upon them.

Although Freedom Hall officially was listed as a "neutral" site for both teams, it was actually UK's home away from home. Fans who couldn't get tickets in Lexington (at Memorial Coliseum, then Rupp Arena) gobbled up the seats in Freedom Hall.

Heck, sometimes 15,000 or so would show up just to watch the Wildcats' "shoot-around" the morning of the game. One year, when the crowd filed away as the Cats left the floor and the higher-ranked Irish took it, Phelps got furious. That sort of provincialism bruised his considerable ego.

So long before his record against UK in Freedom Hall plummeted to 2-9, Phelps was talking loudly about dumping the series at the first available opportunity. He came to hate the Big Blue hoopla, the Big Blue crowd, the Big Blue

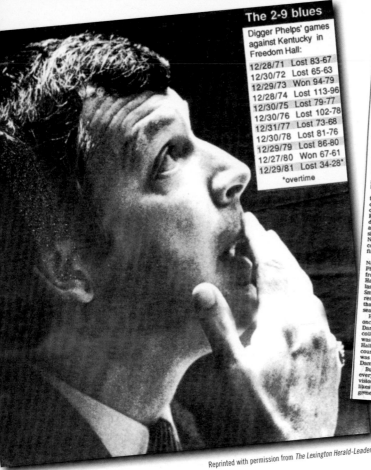

The 2-9 blues

Digger Phelps' games against Kentucky in Freedom Hall:

12/28/71 Lost 83-67
12/30/72 Lost 65-63
12/29/73 Won 94-79
12/28/74 Lost 113-96
12/30/75 Lost 79-77
12/30/76 Lost 102-78
12/31/77 Lost 73-68
12/30/78 Lost 81-76
12/29/79 Lost 86-80
12/27/80 Won 67-61
12/29/81 Lost 34-28*

*overtime

Digger says value of Freedom Hall game diminished

Billy Reed
Courier-Journal sports editor

He will come into Freedom Hall the way he always has — winking, laughing, shaking his head in wonder at the win-crazy University of Kentucky crowd that loves to roar "Sit down, Digger!" whenever he gets up to do a little coaching or pay his respects to an official.

Just because his Notre Dame team has only a 2-4 record, just because the Irish have about as much chance of beating UK as Ronald Reagan has of stopping inflation, don't expect Digger Phelps to be any different Tuesday night. Besides, no matter what happens, the Notre Dame coach will have the comfort of knowing that the agony finally will be over.

Every year since he came to Notre Dame for the 1971-72 season, Phelps has had to bring his team from South Bend, Ind., to Freedom Hall to play UK. His record after last season's 67-61 victory is 2-8. Small wonder that Phelps refused to renew the contract under the terms that have existed since the 1962-63 season.

His predecessor, Johnny Dee, once referred to the UK-Notre Dame game as "The Rose Bowl of college basketball." Of course, that was back in the days when Freedom Hall was the biggest arena in the country. And when the UK game was the biggest payday on Notre Dame's schedule.

But with the advent of new arenas everywhere, new money from television, and new rivalries with the likes of UCLA and DePaul, the UK game shrank in importance from

Notre Dame's point of view. It became just another Big Game — and one in which the Irish were required to compete at a decided disadvantage.

"Because of the old relationship between Adolph (Rupp) and Notre Dame, it (the agreement to play every year in Louisville) happened before I got here," Phelps said yesterday in a telephone interview from South Bend. "That was The Event on the Notre Dame schedule. We could play there for 'X' dollars and it was really important. But a lot has changed in the last 10 years."

Phelps's first season at Notre Dame coincided with Rupp's 41st — and last — at UK. The score that year — UK 83, Notre Dame 67 — set the tone for what has happened to the Irish in Freedom Hall. A few days after that game, Phelps got a phone call from Rupp.

"I thought he was going to tell me something about keeping my spirits up or say something nice about our team," Phelps said, barely suppress-

See IRISH-UK GAME
PAGE 5, col. 1, this section

Staff Photo by C. Thomas Hardin
Notre Dame's Digger Phelps will bring his Irish to Freedom Hall Tuesday for the final time under an existing contract with Kentucky. Next year Kentucky visits the Irish.

Reprinted with permission from *The Courier-Journal*

Reprinted with permission from *The Lexington Herald-Leader*

domination. He especially came to hate the jeering that the Big Blue bigmouths loved to heap on him.

"*Sit downnnnnnnnnnn, Digger!*"

His biggest mistake came in 1976, when he embarrassed UK coach Joe B. Hall with some gibes at a Notre Dame alumni luncheon. The word got back to Hall and that night the Wildcats jumped on Phelps, top-ranked, unbeaten team for a 102-72 victory.

One of the few bright spots for Phelps came on December 27, 1980, when Notre Dame pulled off a 67-61 win over UK. The Irish had a fine team, a national championship contender, built around the trio of Kelly Tripucka, Tracy Jackson, and Orlando Woolridge.

As soon as the game was finished, Phelps stormed across the floor to the press table and began shaking his finger in the face of a Louisville sports columnist who at some point in the distant past had been guilty of implying that Digger's

coaching didn't exactly inspire visions of John Wooden or Adolph Rupp.

"Don't you ever say again that I can't coach," said Phelps, wagging his finger. "This one was for you – for YOU!"

And with that he stormed off to the locker room, leaving

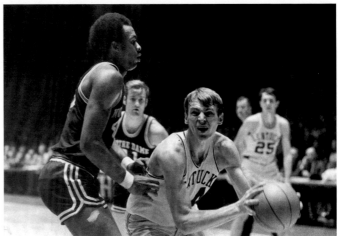

The Courier-Journal
UK star Dan Issel prepares to take it to the hoop against Notre Dame.

Staff Photo by Bill Luster

UK's Jack Givens puts on his warm-up suit as youngsters try to get his autograph at a practice in Louisville.

9,000 pay tribute to No. 1 Cats as UK prepares for the Irish

comment
billy reed

Courier-Journal Sports Editor

Here came James Lee, the people's choice, thundering toward the basket bent on doing one of those patented King Kong dunks that always drives 'em crazy in Lexington's Rupp Arena.

Sure enough, the massive senior forward took the pass, soared toward the hoop and smashed through a two-hander that shook the backboard. Appreciative as ever, the fans jumped up, whistling and applauding, then began to chant "Blue ... Blue ... Blue."

What made this particular moment special was that it didn't happen in a game.

It happened in practice.

Yesterday afternoon, in a rather amazing tribute to the popularity of University of Kentucky basketball, an estimated

9,000 fans left their jobs and homes to come to Freedom Hall to watch the Wildcats, unbeaten and ranked No. 1 in the nation, practice for their nationally televised game this afternoon against Notre Dame, the nation's No. 4 team.

By the time the team arrived at 2:54

p.m., both end zones on the floor were full. So were most of the sections on the sides, all the way to the roof. Outside, many cars were en route to the grounds that traffic on the Watterson pressway was snarled for a mile o

For an hour, the fans sat enra while UK ran through its rather m practice drills. Rick Robey was loud ovation after he went thr dunking exercise. Kyle Macy groans when he missed once in drill. Jay Shidler was cheered fell on the floor, for heaven's s

"This is unbelievable," said s ward Jack (Goose) Givens.

"It's awesome," said coach

"I never saw anything like t

See 9,000 FANS
Back page, col. 1, t

Reprinted with permission from The Courier-Journal

Casey Leads Sputtering UK To 81-73 Win Over Irish With Late Burst of Power

By BILLY REED
Courier-Journal & Times Staff Writer

Well, from the University of Kentucky's point of view, everything came out all right, after all.

UK's basketball team came alive late in the last half to whip Notre Dame 81-73 before a sellout crowd of 17,137 in Freedom Hall last night.

And by his count, and his count only, Adolph Rupp became the winningest college coach of all time. And, finally, sophomore Mike Casey scored 27 points and was voted the game's most valuable player.

But, my, isn't there an easier way?

For the first 31 minutes and 25 seconds of the game, Kentucky looked like anything but one of the nation's top teams.

UK shot only 31 per cent in the first half, then made only two of its first 13 shots in the second half. Its defense was poor. And with 8:35 left in the game, Kentucky trailed Notre Dame 58-48.

Then, with Casey taking charge and th crowd coming alive, Kentucky wrapped up its seventh victory in eight starts with one brilliant burst of offense and defense late in the game.

Here's the way it happened:
With Notre Dame leading 58-48, sopho-

more center Dan Issel scored for UK when Notre Dame's great Bob Whitmore, who wound up with 23 points and 21 rebounds, was called for goal-tending.

Then Notre Dame's Bob Arnzen, who led all scorers with 29 points, missed a jump shot. Casey stole the ball and scored on a layup to bring UK within 58-52 with 7:55 remaining.

Senior center Cliff Berger put in a rebound and Steve Clevenger stole the ball again to set up a fast-break basket by Jim LeMaster on a nice pass from Casey.

10-0 Spree Wins It

LeMaster was called for charging, however, and when Notre Dame's Jim Derrig made a free throw, Kentucky trailed 59-56 with 6:54 left.

Senior Gary Gamble came back with a jumper for UK. Then, after Notre Dame's Dwight Murphy tallied, Kentucky outscored Notre Dame 10-0 in a blitz that won the game.

Gamble started it by stealing the ball at midcourt, then driving for a basket. Berger intercepted a pass and Casey hit a jumper. Then Berger got a rebound and Casey scored on a fast break. Casey's crip shot after a steal and Phil

See CASEY
Page C 4, Col. 3

UK's Mike Casey keeps ball away from defender

Staff Photo by Michael Coers

Reprinted with permission from The Courier-Journal

---

the ink-stained wretch in a somewhat confused state. A day or two later, the scribe wrote that if Digger had, indeed, won the game for him, then he at least deserved the game ball for a keepsake.

Shortly thereafter, a package arrived from South Bend. Inside was a basketball painted with the score: Notre Dame 67, UK 61. But it was not the game ball. At least, not from the 1980 game. It was old and scruffy. If that was the game ball, it must have come from Notre Dame's 19-16 victory in 1929.

In his final appearance against UK in Freedom Hall – on December 29, 1981 – Phelps had one of his finest moments as a coach, no matter what Big Blue fans might have thought to the contrary. Entering the game with an Irish team that was a 17-point underdog in those days before the shot clock, Phelps wisely elected to hold the ball and play keep away.

Instead of pressing the Irish, Hall elected to sit back in a zone defense and let them hold the ball. This led the crowd to jeer Hall as much as Phelps. At one point, a fan came out of the stands, got right next to Hall and yelled in his year, "Press, you idiot!" But Hall didn't budge.

The Irish took UK into overtime before finally losing, 34-28. Although most UK fans cursed and booed him for depriving them of the anticipated blowout, Phelps didn't care. He had the last laugh in Freedom Hall.

When it was mentioned to Phelps that UK-Notre Dame frequently got national television exposure, which helped recruiting on both sides, the Digger snorted.

"In all the years we've played in Louisville," he said, "the crowd there is the issue. I don't care how many millions are watching on TV. With 19,000 yelling at us, it's always a road game."

After Phelps announced that Notre Dame would no longer play UK in Freedom Hall every December, Hall determined that he wasn't about to go to South Bend every other year and expose himself to the kind of taunting that Phelps got in Louisville. So the UK-Notre Dame series was allowed to expire after the Wildcats went to South Bend for a token 1982 appearance and survived with a 58-45 victory.

The last UK-Notre Dame game in Freedom Hall came on January 31, 1988. The Wildcats won, 78-69, to improve their all-time Louisville record against Notre Dame to 24-7. In Freedom Hall, it was UK 21, Notre Dame 4. From then on, the teams played in Lexington, South Bend, and the Big Four Classic in Indianapolis.

On December 11, 1971, Freedom Hall was the scene of a game that proved to be more important, historically, than anybody could have guessed at the time. It was a meeting between Adolph Rupp's last Kentucky team and Bob Knight's first Indiana team. After the season, Rupp would be forced into retirement with 876 career victories, a record that some thought would never be broken.

However, North Carolina's Dean Smith passed him in 1997 and retired with 879 victories. But Knight passed both and had 902 victories to his credit when he resigned at Texas Tech late in the 2008 season. For the record, Knight had 102 wins at West Point, 662 at Indiana, and 138 at Texas Tech.

Knight was no stranger to Freedom Hall. He had been a junior on the 1961 defending NCAA champion Ohio State team that defeated Kentucky, 87-74, in the finals of the Mideast Regional tournament. A year later, Knight was a senior reserve on the Buckeye team that lost to Cincinnati in the NCAA championship game.

Billy Reed

Instead of replacing Adolph Rupp at UK, ex-Wildcat and Boston Celtic star Frank Ramsey (left) spent some time coaching the Kentucky Colonels of the ABA.

University of Kentucky Audio-Visual Archives

Adolph Rupp (left) and longtime assistant Harry Lancaster.

After becoming the head coach at West Point in 1965 – at 24, he was the youngest head coach in the nation – Knight brought his team – to Freedom Hall to play Louisville. The game had been arranged by *Louisville Times* sports editor Dean Eagle in order to give local fans the treat of seeing two outstanding Louisville high school products – senior Army center Mike Silliman of St. Xavier and sophomore U of L center Wes Unseld of Seneca – square off against each other as collegians. Both were 6-6, short for center, but both were rebounding demons.

Playing before a crowd of 13,000, Silliman had a nice homecoming, scoring 30 points to go with nine rebounds. But Louisville won the game easily, 84-56, thanks mainly to Unseld's 22 points and 18 rebounds. Said Knight, "We just got the (bleep) stomped out of us from the opening tip." Silliman went on to become the captain of the 1968 U.S. Olympic team while Unseld, after graduating from Louisville in '68, became the first player in NBA history to be rookie of the year and Most Valuable Player in the same season.

So now here was Knight again, taking on a legend whose teams he had followed on 50,000-watt Louisville radio

station WHAS while growing up in Orrville, Ohio. At the time of their meeting in Freedom Hall, Rupp was 69, Knight 31. Rupp wore his trademark brown suit, Knight a plaid sport coat with his tied loosened. Rupp was the father of fast-break offense basketball, Knight a proponent of man-to-man defense that amounted to hand-to-hand combat.

On this night, however, Knight won playing Rupp's game, but not before the teams battled through 40 tough minutes of regulation and two overtimes. The Wildcats couldn't stop Indiana's 6-8 Steve Downing, who scored 47 points to go with 25 rebounds, and Knight's defense didn't have much better luck with UK's Jim Andrews, who had 22 points and 13 rebounds. Finally, Indiana prevailed, 90-89, in a game that left the crowd of 17,269 limp with exhaustion.

"That game made a connection for our new program with old-line Indiana fans," said Knight in the 2002 autobiography he did with veteran Bloomington sports editor Bob Hammel. "Downing was heroic. The cartilage problem in the knee he had injured the week before slowed him down, but he played. He played all 50 minutes. In

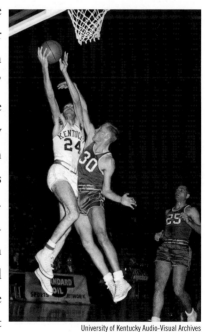

University of Kentucky Audio-Visual Archives

Johnny Cox (24) led UK to the 1958 NCAA title in Freedom Hall.

Indiana, they make legends of performances like that one, in a basketball victory over Kentucky. Hell, it *was* legendary."

And so began what became arguably the best non-conference rivalry in the nation for the next 30 years. When Knight left Indiana after the 1999-2000 season, he had a 15-17 record against Kentucky. In Freedom Hall, the Wildcats had a 4-3 edge over Knight, who was 1-0 against Rupp in Louisville, 2-0 against Joe B. Hall, 0-2 against Rick Pitino, and 0-1 against Tubby Smith.

The infamous "cuffing" incident between Bob Knight (right) and Joe B. Hall in 1974.

Freedom Hall is where Joe B. Hall saved his career as Kentucky's head coach during a remarkable three-game stretch in December, 1974.

.After replacing Adolph Rupp after the 1971-'72 season, Hall's first two seasons in Lexington were indifferent, at best. His first team, led by "Super Sophs" Kevin Grevey, Jimmy Dan Conner, Mike Flynn and Bob Guyette, completed a good, but not, great, 20-8 season by losing to Indiana in the finals of the Mideast Regional.

His second team dipped to a shocking 13-13, tying Rupp's worst record in 41 seasons, and raised serious doubts about whether Hall was up to the task of filling the Baron's shoes. His third team was the one that would make or break Hall. The "Super Sophs" now were seniors, and they were joined by a blue-ribbon freshman class that included two 6-11 kids, Rick Robey and Mike Phillips, and two high school phenoms from Lexington, Jack Givens and James Lee.

After a couple of easy wins at home, the Wildcats went to Bloomington and got hammered by Indiana, 98-74. With a lineup consisting of UK recruit Kent Benson at center, Scott May and Steve Green at forwards, and Quinn Buckner and Bobby Wilkerson at guards, the Hoosiers dominated in every respect.

Late in the game, with UK hopelessly behind, Knight cuffed Hall on the back of the head as they stood next to each other on the sidelines. Although Knight later said the gesture was meant to be playful, Hall took it as a lack of respect. It seemed like piling on, insult added to injury.

Cawood Ledford interviewing Joe B. Hall.

The victory gave Knight a 3-0 record against Hall and led some Wildcat fans to believe that Hall wasn't in the same class with the brash young coach in Bloomington. Next up for Kentucky was hardly a get-well game -- North Carolina in Freedom Hall. The Tar Heels had a star-studded lineup that included Phil Ford, Tom LaGarde, John Kuester, Walter Davis, and Mitch Kupchak.

Early on, the Tar Heels looked as if they were going to dominate UK every bit as much as Indiana had, steaming to a 31-16 lead. On the UK bench, Hall became so upset that he threw off his sports coat and stomped on it. The problem was, he forgot he was wearing contact lenses and that his glasses were in the coat pocket.

But then Jimmy Dan Conner, a former Kentucky Mr. Basketball from Anderson County, stepped in to lead a 26-3 surge that put the Wildcats in control. With Conner hitting 15 of 21 from the floor and scoring 35 points, the Wildcats went on to win, 90-78, and momentarily muffled Hall's critics.

After returning home to win the UK Invitational Tournament with easy wins over Washington State and Oklahoma State, the Wildcats returned to Freedom Hall for their next big test, this one against Kansas. Buoyed by a roaring crowd of 13,144, the Cats rode Grevey's 29 points to a 100-63 victory, proving the North Carolina win hadn't been a fluke.

Only five days later, they returned to Freedom Hall to play Notre Dame and were greeted by a crowd of 16,615, the largest to see them play that season. On paper, the Irish had about as much talent as anybody in the country, led by husky forward Adrian Dantley, the nation's No. 2 scorer the previous season. Phelps surrounded him two strong 6-9 rebounders, Dave Batton and Toby Knight; 6-6 swingman Bill Paterno; and 6-2 floor leader Dwight Clay.

With Notre Dame leading 36-28, the Cats went on a 15-0 run that was sparked by substitute guard Larry Johnson. Much to the Digger's chagrin, his team folded like a cheap tent. At the end, Kentucky had a 113-96 victory and

University of Kentucky Audio-Visual Archives
NBC's Al McGuire (right) interviews Dwight Anderson (center) and Joe B. Hall after a 1978 win over Notre Dame.

five players in double figures, led by Grevey's 28, Guyette's 18, and Johnson's 16. With a game-high 39, Dantley was marvelous for the Irish.

The three-game sweep in Freedom Hall put UK on the road to the Southeastern Conference championship and a rematch against Indiana – top-ranked and unbeaten – in the NCAA Mideast championship game in Dayton. Although the Hoosiers were hampered by an arm injury that limited All-American May to only a token appearance, they battled UK to the end before losing, 92-90. Besides avenging the debacle in December, the Wildcats earned Hall his first Final Four trip and got a lot of the Rupp monkey off his back. On the bus ride home from Dayton, UK fans lined the overpasses on Interstate-75 to salute the teams with banners and cheers.

Later that same calendar year, the teams met again in Freedom Hall under decidedly different circumstances. While Indiana had lost only Green from the '75 team, Kentucky had lost Grevey, Conner, Flynn, and Guyette. It was a foregone conclusion that Knight, still devastated by the loss in Dayton, would try to punish the Cats if he could.

The Courier-Journal

Mike Pratt scored 42 against the Irish in 1969. He now does analysis for the UK Radio Network.

But thanks mainly to sophomore Givens, who would finish with 20 points,

Kentucky was having none of it. Cheered on by a pro-UK crowd of 16,615, the Wildcats had a 64-62 lead and

possession of the ball inside the final 30 seconds. Following a miss by Johnson, Indiana rebounded and got the ball to May, who put up a shot that missed. Amazingly, however, Benson, who was falling down, managed to slap the ball into the basket to send the game into overtime.

Given a reprieve, the Hoosiers took care of business, outscored the Cats 13-4 for a 77-68 win that easily could have been a loss. As it turned out, that was as close as the Hoosiers came to losing in a 32-0 season that culminated with the first of Knight's three NCAA championships.

Until Jodie Meeks torched Appalachian State for 46 in December, 2008, the individual UK scoring record in Freedom Hall was owned by Mike Pratt, who scored 42 in a 110-90 rout of Notre Dame on December 28, 1969. A 6-4 junior from Dayton, Pratt played amateur baseball with Mike Schmidt, who went on to become a baseball Hall-of-Famer with the Philadelphia Phillies.

Rupp liked Pratt for his rebounding and his unselfishness. For his first two years, Pratt was content to let classmates Dan Issel and Mike Casey get most of the headlines. But when injuries suffered in a car accident sidelined Casey for the 1969-'70 season, Pratt stepped up and played second fiddle to Issel, the 6-9 scoring machine who still ranks as UK's all-time leading men's scorer – even though he only played three varsity seasons.

But no Big Blue player ever electrified a Freedom Hall crowd quite like another Dayton product -- 6-3 Dwight Anderson. As a freshman, Anderson came off the bench against Notre Dame on December 29, 1980, and scored 17 second-half points as the Wildcats overcome a 12-point deficit to win, 86-80. Former Marquette Coach Al McGuire, calling the game for NBC with Dick Enberg and Billy Packer, dubbed Anderson "The Blur" and said he had never seen anybody who could move faster with the ball.

After the Notre Dame series ended in 1982, Kentucky didn't have a regular opponent in Freedom Hall. Beginning in

UK alum Jack Guthrie (left) presents a trophy to Coach Hall after 83-62 win over Kansas in 1982.

1983, it played Louisville every other year on the Cardinals' home floor (see UK-U of L chapter), and it played Indiana in Freedom Hall every other year from 1992 through 2004.

Otherwise, though, only Kansas and Austin Peay (twice each) have played UK in Freedom Hall more than once. The one-time opponents have included Purdue, VMI, Georgia, Austin Peay, North Carolina, Western Kentucky, Morehead State, Ole Miss, Marshall, Alabama, Georgia Tech, Tulane, Iona, Chattanooga, Alabama-Birmingham, and Appalachian State.

As college budgets have risen to proportions that couldn't have been imagined in Rupp's day, athletics directors have been under growing pressure to schedule as many home games as possible. In UK's case, home games in 23,500-seat Rupp Arena mean bigger paydays than "neutral" games in 19,000-seat Freedom Hall.

Nevertheless, no UK athletics director has been willing to break a tradition that has been good both for the program and its fan base. Going back to 1936, the Wildcats have played at least one game in Louisville almost every season. In the old Armory, they won seven SEC tournament championships from 1941 through 1952.

As part of the University's of Louisville's deal with the new downtown arena, due to open in 2010, the Wildcats will not be allowed to play there unless they're in an NCAA tournament game. That means that for the foreseeable future, if UK wants to continue playing in Louisville, Freedom Hall will be its home away from home.

In the spring of 2009, new UK Coach John Calipari said he wouldn't be averse to renewing the series with Notre Dame, alternating the games between Freedom Hall and the Conseco Fieldhouse in Indianapolis. He also favored moving the UK-Indiana series from campus to Freedom Hall and Conseco Fieldhouse in Indianapolis.

"Let's do it!" said Calipari, endearing himself to the large Big Blue fan base in Jefferson County. "Now that we have our own arena in Louisville, we want to play several games here."

TRACK AND FIELD

When the Mason-Dixon Games began in 1961, track-and-field stars were so enamored with Freedom Hall's setup – especially the banked track, which was very conducive for world records – that Louisville almost immediately became a must-stop on the indoor circuit. Over the years, such Olympic luminaries as sprinter Wilma Rudolph, pole-vaulter Billy Olson, hurdler Renaldo Nehemiah, long-jumper Ralph Boston, and distance runner Steve Scott have appeared in Freedom Hall.

But when amateur sports changed its rules in the 1970s

and began allowing athletes to take money from shoe companies and event sponsors, the Mason-Dixon Games began to fall on hard times, mostly because the event didn't have the cash to keep pace with what the athletes were getting in larger cities.

In 1978, for example, Mason-Dixon Games official Charlie Ruter found himself in a car with a world-class high jumper. Ruter asked the athlete if he might be interested in competing in Louisville. The athlete immediately ticked off his demands: Round-trip air fare from Miami, all expenses,

Famed hurdler Renaldo Nehmiah (right) shows his form in the Mason-Dixon Games.

Photo courtesy of Charlie Ruter

Track official Charlie Ruter with immortal Olympic star Wilma Rudolph.

and an extra $300 to $500 for just showing up.

"I could only wish him good luck," Charlie Ruter said. "At the time, the Mason-Dixon Games only had around $15,000 to pay athletes. That was less than half what was being spent by the Millrose Games in New York."

For years, Ruter was the heart and soul behind the Mason-Dixon Games. He attended Western Kentucky State Teachers College (now University) and played basketball for the legendary E.A. Diddle. However, Ruter was interested in all sports, not just basketball, and track and field became his passion.

A decorated Naval hero who saw combat in the South Pacific in World War II, Ruter returned to Tokyo in 1964 as an official with the U.S. Olympic team. As the American team marched into the Olympic stadium, the only person ahead of Ruter was hurdler Edwin Moses, carrying the U.S. flag.

"Here I am in Tokyo where I entered as a conquering hero and the people turned their backs," he once said, "but now here they were, standing and cheering. Surely, this must be the pinnacle for a track official. I know of no greater honor I could receive."

He received another pretty good one at the 1984 games in Los Angeles, when he was put in charge of selecting the officials who would work the track-and-field events. Together, Ruter and the indoor track at Freedom Hall put Louisville on the international track-and-field map.

Besides the Mason-Dixon games, Ruter was a fixture at the Freedom Hall press table, serving as official scorer on a team that also included public-address announcer John Tong and timer Richard "Rosie" Rozel. They worked games for U of L, the Kentucky Colonels, and the NCAA when it brought the Final Four to town.

In February, 1980, a half-dozen Russian athletes competed in the Mason-Dixon Games, the fourth stop in a five-city tour that ended in Houston. The Russians were escorted into the arena by a quartet of uniformed Kentucky State Troopers due to the international tension that existed over the Russian invasion of Afghanistan.

The Russian delegation was led by David Peztenawa, minister of sport for the Soviet republic of Georgia. He was a full-time employee of the state, he said, and charged with administering sports for the thousands of athletes who were training in Georgia. He said basketball was a growing sport in Russia, so he was especially pleased to get a first-hand view of historic Freedom Hall. He said that Tbilisi, the capital of Georgia, had three modern indoor arenas for track and field, but none for basketball as big or nice as Freedom Hall.

Told that the Russian national team had played the University of Louisville a few months earlier, Peztenawa said, "And what was the result?" Told the Russians had won easily, he smiled and nodded.

Photo courtesy of Charlie Ruter

Announcer John Tong (left) and Charlie Ruter worked a lot of track events together.

The Russians stood at attention during the playing of the U.S. national anthem at the start of the meet, and then went out to do their jobs. Hurdler Katya Smirnova was runner-up to Stephanie Hightower of Louisville and Ohio State in the 60-meter hurdles, with another Russian third.

Only a couple of weeks later, President Jimmy Carter announced that the U.S. was boycotting the 1980 Olympics in Moscow because Russia hadn't pulled its troops out of Afghanistan. The Russians returned the favor in 1984, boycotting the Olympics in Los Angeles.

In 1972, a couple of international heroes squared off in the most ballyhooed human race ever held in Freedom Hall. It was American Jim Ryun against Kenyan Kip Keino in a professional meet sponsored by the International Track Association.

Their 1,500-meters matchup was the most exciting event going into the 1968 Olympic Games in Mexico City. Ryun was the handsome American record-breaker from Kansas, Keino the indefatigable long-distance man from Kenya. They were on the cover of *Sports Illustrated*'s pre-Olympics issue.

As it turned out, their duel dissolved when Ryun pulled up lame and pulled himself out of the race, leaving Keino an easy path to the gold medal. But nobody was much disappointed because of other newsworthy events, such as sprinters Tommy Davis and John Carlos hanging their heads and holding up black-gloved fists on the victory stand to protest racism in America and the war in Vietnam.

Still, there was an unfinished, to-be-continued feeling to the Ryun-Keino duel. Ryun fans remained unconvinced that Keino was better. Keino fans contended the outcome in Mexico City would have been the same had Ryun stayed healthy.

Before the race in Freedom Hall, Keino sat on the sidelines and said, as he laced up his shoes, "I like the track…it's so beeeg." Indeed, the banked track in Freedom Hall had eight laps to a mile, while others have as many as 11 or 12.

After the crowd gave Ryan and Keino the warmest receptions of the night, the gun sounded to start the race. Through the first six laps, the lead was held by Keith Munson, the only other runner in the race.

Then, with a lap and a half to go, Ryun made his move. Slack-jawed, head bobbing side-to-side, occasionally sneaking glances at Keino over his right shoulder, Ryun took the lead.

The question in the last lap was whether Keino would be able to overtake the flying figure of Ryun. The answer was no. As Ryun crossed the finish line in 4:01.9, no world record, Keino still was a good five or six yards behind.

But Keino didn't seem disappointed. As always, he seemed to delight in the simple exhilaration of competition. So while Ryun slowly walked around the track, head hanging, Keino pranced lightly on the balls of his feet. And when they turned the spotlight on him, he responded with another big smile and a wave.

"People in Kenya love Keino," said a friend, Oliver Warobi. "We call him our 'ambassador of athletics' because he's won so many friends for Kenya by running around the world."

The mile run, glamour event of any track-and-field meet, was only 30 minutes or so away, and under the stands at Freedom Hall, out of the audience's sight, the milers were shaking the soreness and weariness out of their muscles as they got ready to compete in the 1979 Mason-Dixon Games.

The bald guy with the mustache was Dick Buerkle, the Colorado contact-lens salesmen who then held the world indoor record (3:54.9). His face was set in a frown, as if his feet hurt. He admitted later that he didn't feel well due to a cold.

The lanky guy with the TV-anchorman good looks was Marty Liquori, long one of America's premier distance runners. When he was not running, Liquori sold sporting goods and did part-time work for the ABC network. He looked loose and relaxed as he loped along.

And the guy with the lank brown hair and jutting chin was Ray Flynn, a native of Ireland and a product of East Tennessee State. He trotted along with quick, mincing little steps. He and Liquori both wore the blue-and-white warmups of the Athletic Attic team of Gainesville, Florida.

Flynn figured to be the favorite, based on his performances so far that year, but the crowd of around 6,000 barely noticed him when the runners strolled into the arena and began taking their final warm-up laps around the sweeping Freedom Hall track.

As soon as they caught sight of Buerkle's shaved dome, the paying customers began to yell and applaud. Liquori, too, was easy to identify because of his TV exposure. So he also drew plenty of attention as he jogged around.

The crowd expected a mile under four minutes – perhaps even one faster than Filbert Bayi's 1977 meet record of 3:57.2.

Mason-Dixon Games

Olympic distance star Marty Liquori lost to Ray Flynn in the 1979 Mason-Dixon Games.

The Freedom Hall track is bigger than most – eight laps to a mile instead of 10 or more – and the field was as good as any indoor meet in the country would draw that year.

The Mason-Dixon officials, who are nationally respected

for their knowledge and competence, got the milers to the starting line right on time. Promptly at 9:20 p.m., the starter's gun exploded and Wayne Colley, who had entered only to assure a record-breaking pace, bolted to the lead.

Colley went as hard as he could as long as he could, racing through a quarter-mile in 58 seconds and a half-mile in 1:58 before giving way to Flynn. But just as Flynn swept past him to take the lead, something starting happened at the rear of the pack: Buerkle suddenly pulled up, stepped off the track, and began putting on his warm-ups.

"I wasn't feeling that well after three laps," he said later. "I was gasping. I could have kept on going, but I would have finished 30 seconds behind, and I didn't want to disappoint the crowd or get booed, so I stopped."

The crowd got over its surprise in a hurry and concentrated on Flynn, who was opening a big lead—10 yards, then 20. With Buerkle on the sidelines, the only guy on the track with the slightest chance of catching Flynn was Liquori. He moved into second after six laps, but knew it would take a miracle to catch Flynn.

"I went out too fast, right on the pace-setter's shoulders," Liquori said later. "When I eased up and fell back into the middle of the back, I had three guys on me. I had to pass them, and, by that time, Flynn was gone. He got a pretty good lead in the middle of the race."

Flynn hit the tape in 3:58.9, almost two seconds and 15 yards ahead of Liquori. It was the fastest mile of his career, but he said he could have run even faster if he had been pushed.

Fast enough to challenge Buerkle's world record?

"Oh, I don't know," Flynn said. "That's a tough world record."

A year later, Flynn returned to Louisville to defend his Mason-Dixon title. Buerkle also returned, hoping to redeem himself with the Freedom Hall crowd. But Liquori was replaced by John Walker of New Zealand, who had won the

New Zealand's John Walker won the mile at the 1980 Mason-Dixon Games.

1,500-meter run at the 1976 Olympics and held the world mile record for a time.

Three days before the meet in Louisville, Walker and countryman Rod Dixon, a specialist in the 3,000-meter run, left Australia for New York. They caught a few hours rest there before coming on to Louisville, their first stop on a three-city swing of indoor meets.

"We intended to work out," Walker said, "but we were just too tired. We went to our rooms and went to sleep. I woke up and said, 'Where are we?' All I know about Louisville is this is where the Kentucky Derby is held. Somebody told me it was nice and warm here, too."

As soon as the race started, Martyn Brewer, recruited by Mason-Dixon officials to ensure a fast early pace, dashed to the lead and led the field through the first quarter-mile in :58.7. Flynn was a distant second, with Walker on his elbow in third. Buerkle brought up the rear.

It was fitting that New Zealand's Rod Dixon would impress the Freedom Hall crowd at the Mason-Dixon Games.

At the half, which was timed in 1:59, the order was the same. But then Brewer stopped and stepped off the track, his job done, and Walker swept to the lead. After passing the three-quarters mark in exactly three minutes, the New Zealander began to pick up the pace. On the gun lap, he looked over his shoulders to see Flynn and Indiana University's Jim Spivey coming after him.

But it was too little, too late. Walker hit the finish line in 3:57.7, best indoor time for a mile in the United States so far that year and only a half-second off Bayi's meet record.

"If I'd known I was that close," Walker said, "I'd have kicked a little harder. Running indoors is so bloody hard for me. I weigh nearly 165 pounds and that's a lot heavier than the average indoor runner. Those boards gave me a beating."

A few moments later, Dixon took the 3,000 meters to give the New Zealanders a sweep. Smiling impishly, Dixon said, "I've always said that the one games in America that I wanted to go to were the Mason-Dixon Games. I suppose I like the Dixon part of it."

Nearby, Walker smiled.

"Next year," he said, "we want the name changed to the Walker-Dixon Games."

For the record, neither Walker nor Dixon won a gold medal at the 1980 Olympics in Moscow. And by 2009, the world indoor mile record had been reduced to 3:48.45 by Hicham El Guerrouj of Morocco.

THE CARDINALS' HOME NEST

A sold-out crowd soon after Freedom Hall opened in 1956.

When the University of Louisville men's basketball team leaves the Freedom Hall floor after the final home game of the 2009-'10 season, it will end a 54-year era in which the arena played a major role in helping the Cardinals develop into a perennial national power. From the 1956-'57 season until the early 1970s, Freedom Hall's 16,600-seat capacity for basketball gave U of L the biggest home arena in the nation. But then the steady rise of college basketball's popularity inspired an unprecedented building boom.

By the time Tennessee opened its 24,575-seat Stokely

Center in 1987, Freedom Hall had been surpassed in capacity by several arenas, most notably Indiana's Assembly Hall (18,000), Brigham Young's Marriott Center (22,700), Kentucky's Rupp Arena (23,500), and the Syracuse Carrier Dome (33,000).

Besides that, several cities, encouraged by the success of Houston's multi-purpose Astrodome (site of the 1971 NCAA Final Four), began building domed stadiums. The 1982 Final Four was held in the Louisiana Superdome in New Orleans, beginning a trend away from conventional arenas to domes. The last Final Four held in a conventional arena was the 1996 event won by Kentucky at the Meadowlands in New Jersey.

John Dromo (right) was Hickman's longtime assistant and successor.

Initially, Bernard "Peck" Hickman, Louisville's coach from 1944 through 1969, was skeptical about playing in Freedom Hall. He didn't see any way his team, which averaged about 9,000 fans per game in the downtown Armory, could come close to filling up the cavern on a regular basis. However, he changed his tune after the Cardinals drew well for three 1956-'57 games in the new building – 13,756 for Notre Dame, 15,400 for St. Louis, and 11,900 for Dayton.

"It would be wonderful," said Hickman, "to have the facilities at the state fairgrounds for our permanent use. No school could touch us for game facilities. Maybe we should move all our games to Freedom Hall next year."

Which they did.

Unfortunately, attendance was disappointing, an average of only about 8,000 per game, because the Cardinals (1) were coming off a 13-12 season, (2) were in the second year of NCAA probation for recruiting violations, and (3) had lost Charlie Tyra, their consensus All-American center who had led them to the 1956 NIT championship.

When the Cards opened the 1958-'59 season in Freedom Hall, they were shocked by Georgetown, Kentucky, College, 84-78, before a crowd of only 5,500. That was a decidedly inauspicious beginning to a season that ended up with the Cardinals being the first – and still the only – team to play in the Final Four on their home court.

Going into February, the Cards were only 9-9. On February 4, they had to play Florida Southern in the Armory because of a scheduling conflict at Freedom Hall

Bernard "Peck" Hickman coached the Cardinals from 1944-1967.

a 76-61 victory. Then they defeated Michigan State to earn their first trip to the Final Four, which was being played in Freedom Hall for the second consecutive year (see Final Fours chapter).

University of Louisville Sports Information

In 1963, U of L became the first university south of the Mason-Dixon line to integrate its basketball team.

University of Louisville Sports Information

Charlie Tyra led the Cardinals to the 1956 NIT Championship.

and presented Hickman with his 400th career victory, 88-57. Maybe the return to its old haunt settled the Cards, and maybe it didn't, but the team nevertheless won 10 of 11 games to earn an NCAA at-large bid.

After opening NCAA play with a 77-63 win over Eastern Kentucky on UK's home court in Lexington, the 17-10 Cardinals advanced to Evanston, Illinois, to meet Rupp's Wildcats, who were 23-2 and ranked second in the nation. It was only U of L's second appearance in the NCAA tournament and their first since 1950-'51, when they lost to UK, 79-68, in the Eastern Regional in Raleigh, North Carolina.

After spotting the Wildcats a 29-14 lead, the Cardinals rallied to within 36-28 at halftime. The second half was no contest. With Don Goldstein (19 points, 13 rebounds) and John Turner (13 points, eight rebounds) leading the way, the Cards thumped the Cats 48-25 in the second half for

After four consecutive so-so years – 15-10, 21-8, 15-10, and 14-11 – the Cardinals made national news in 1963-'64 by becoming the first predominantly white university south of the Mason-Dixon line to break the color barrier. The pioneers were sophomores Sam Smith of Hazard, Wade Houston of Alcoa, Tennessee, and Eddie Whitehead of Lincoln Heights, Ohio.

In the Cards' opening game, a 113-82 romp over Georgetown in Freedom Hall, none of the African-Americans started. But Smith was the first sub, replacing center Judd Rothmann with 12:25 remaining in the first half. A crowd of 7,160 warmly applauded each of the three black players throughout the game.

Although Whitehead didn't score, the 6-6 Smith acquitted himself well with 11 points and seven rebounds. And Houston made five of eight from the floor, including a 20-footer late in the game to give the Cards 100 points.

On January 18, because of a mobile-home show in Freedom Hall, the Cards were forced to play Georgia Tech in the Armory, which had been spruced up and re-named the Convention Center. The Cards came from behind to win, 68-59, to begin a six-game winning streak that left them at 14-5.

On February 4, however, both Smith and Whitehead were declared academically ineligible. "Not only did Sam Smith flunk out," said U of L assistant John Dromo, "but the tutor we hired to work with him flunked out, too."

The loss of Smith, who was coming off a 24-point, 10-rebound performance against DePaul, hurt the Cards down the stretch. They won only one of their last five games to finish at 15-9, but still got an at-large NCAA bid and a spot against Ohio University in the first round.

University of Louisville Sports Information
Wes Unseld spurned UK's Adolph Rupp to sign with U of L in 1964.

Forced to leave two more players at home due to academic deficiencies (Bobby Doutaz and Larry Holman), the Cards nevertheless took the Bobcats into overtime before losing, 71-69.

After the season, Hickman scored the biggest recruiting coup of his career, beating out Kentucky, UCLA, and many

other top programs for Westley Unseld, the 6-6 center who had led Seneca High to back-to-back state titles in 1963 and '64. Since freshmen were ineligible in those days, Unseld had to sit and watch while the 1964-'65 Cards struggled to a 15-10 record, the fifth time in six years that U of L had failed to win more than 15 games.

In the spring of that year, the Cards once more beat out Kentucky, UCLA and many other top schools for the state's No. 1 prospect – Breckinridge County's 6-3 Butch Beard, who had led his team to the 1965 state championship.

University of Louisville Sports Information
Butch Beard was the prototype of the modern guard: big and quick.

Besides being U of L's first African-American stars, Unseld and Beard had the talent to attract unprecedented national attention to the program. An unmovable force around the basket, Unseld also triggered the Cards' fast break with the meanest outlet pass in college basketball. He set impregnable picks off which Beard drove or pulled up for a jumper.

Alas, however, the Unseld-Beard era proved to be only bittersweet. Unseld's sophomore team in 1965-'66 went 16-10 and lost in the first round of the NIT. In 1966-'67, with Unseld as a junior and Beard a sophomore, the Cards went 23-5 and were ranked second to UCLA in the wire-service polls, only to be shocked by SMU, 83-81, in the NCAA Midwest Regional semifinals.

Under heat from the public and the press, Hickman announced his retirement on July 17, 1967, and turned the

Nobody could stop the burly Unseld when he went to the boards.

John Dromo was a formidable recruiter.

team over to Dromo, his assistant for 19 seasons. Dromo's assistants would be Howard Stacey and T.L. Plain. Most Cardinal fans figured the change would be just what the team would need to make a serious title run in 1967-'68, when Unseld would be a senior and Beard a junior.

In the Cardinals' opening game, Unseld scored 45 points in a 118-86 win over Georgetown College to break Bud Olsen's single-game scoring record by a point. With 11 of its next 13 games on the road, the Cards had their work cut out for them, especially considering that Beard looked uncomfortable at guard and running mate

South Carolina transfer Mike Grosso was a force around the hoop.

Fred Holden was nagged by knee injuries.

Shockingly, the Cards lost to Northwestern in Chicago Stadium, Dayton in Dayton Arena, Kansas in Freedom Hall, Columbia in Madison Square Garden, Bradley in Peoria, and Cincinnati in the Cincinnati Gardens. The team expected to battle UCLA for the national title found itself at 8-6 on January 23.

But then came a 12-game winning streak that culminated with a 107-58 victory over Bellarmine on March 4. In his last home game, Unseld had 30 points and 23 rebounds. He was backed up by 6-9 South Carolina transfer Mike Grosso, who had 11 points and 10 boards.

"In December," said Dromo, "I wondered if anybody would show up at our banquet. This has been one of the most gratifying years of my life. We have learned that good things don't come easy."

Alas for the Cards, their first NCAA opponent was 29-0 Houston, which had wrested the No. 1 ranking away from Lew Alcindor and UCLA with a nationally-televised 71-69 win over the Bruins in the Houston Astrodome. The Cougars were led by Elvin "The Big E" Hayes and outstanding guard Don Chaney.

After jumping out to a 13-11 lead, the Cards crumbled before a 26-4 Houston onslaught. During that stretch, U of

L made only one of 16 shots. Ahead by 37-17, Hayes and his teammates waved bye-bye and rolled to a 91-75 victory. Unseld was brilliant with 23 points and 22 rebounds, but Hayes, with 35 points and 24 rebounds, was other-worldly.

Without Unseld, Beard's senior team lost the Missouri Valley Conference championship to Drake and ended up in the NIT, where it defeated Fordham and lost to Boston College for a final 21-6 record. Amazingly, Beard and fellow seniors Jerry King, Dennis Deeken, and Ed Lionis enjoyed a phenomenal 39-1 record in Freedom Hall during their three varsity seasons.

Forced to regroup in 1969-'70, Dromo surrounded the 6-9 Grosso with five players who were known as the "Super Sophs" – Jim Price, Henry Bacon, Al Vilcheck, Mike Lawhon,

The Courier-Journal

In 1972, guard Jim Price directed the Cards to the NCAA Final Four.

and Larry Carter. Although none of them individually was as coveted a prospect as Unseld or Beard, together they formed the best recruiting class in Cardinal history.

After getting off to a 16-4 start, however, the young Cards collapsed down the stretch, losing five of their last season games – including a loss to Oklahoma in the first round of the NIT – to finish 18-9. "In my 30 years of coaching," Dromo told his team after the final game, "I've never been so mad. It's not just this game. It's the whole season."

The Cards got off to an 8-1 start in 1970-'71 and seemed poised for a serious run at the Final Four. But on January 2, 1971, after an 86-84 win at Tulsa, Dromo was taken to St. Francis Hospital because of a rapidly beating heart and suffered a major heart attack while under sedation. Only 54, Dromo almost died. The next day, Peck Hickman, now U of L's athletics director, informed assistant Howard Stacey that he would be interim coach for the remainder of the season.

Only 31, Stacey was known as the "Silver Fox" because of his prematurely gray hair. He had played for Hickman in the early '70s and was married to former U of L cheerleader Judy Heldman, whose father had coached U of L from 1940-'42 before taking over as athletics director.

Under Stacey, the Cards were only so-so, posting a 9-6 record to stand at 18-7 for the season heading into their final home game against Memphis State, also 18-7. In conference play, both the Cards and Tigers were 8-5, meaning each needed a victory to move into a three-team playoff with Drake and St. Louis for the conference title and the league's automatic NCAA bid.

Before the game, Dromo told anybody who would listen that he was coming back the following season, even though he knew he wasn't. But he didn't want Stacey to get the job since he knew that Stacey already had engaged in secret talks with Drake about replacing Maury John in Des Moines.

With 11:36 to play in the first half, Louisville's Mike Lawhon, a part-time Sunday school teacher, elbowed Memphis State's James Douglas as the two were starting up the floor after a missed shot. Douglas retaliated with a forearm that decked Lawhon and led the officials to call a timeout.

On the way to their benches, Lawhon and Douglas exchanged words, at which point Memphis State's Fred Horton stepped between the two and pushed Lawhon. And so began the darnedest free-for-all anybody had seen at a U of L basketball since the Cards and Seton Hall had duked it out at the old Armory in 1953.

As the fisticuffs were starting to recede on the floor, Horton went to the press table, grabbed a folding metal chair, and began waving it at the U of L players. Then he climbed up on the table and began swinging it at anyone who approached.

While almost everyone was watching Horton, Memphis State reserve Doug McKinney snuck up behind U of L's Price and gouged him in the eye. As Price doubled up, holding his hands over his eyes, Bacon came after McKinney, chasing him into the stands and stalking him from section to section.

Bacon's attention was finally diverted when Horton, swinging the chair at Louisville's Ron Thomas, missed and hit Memphis assistant Wayne Yates under an eye, opening a cut that required stitches. That gave McKinney an opening to dart out of the stands to the Memphis bench, where he watched police swoop in on Horton, take the chair away from him, and tie his hands behind him.

When play was finally resumed, Lawhon, of all people, made two technical free throws to push Louisville ahead. At the start of the second half, the Cards outscored Memphis 15-1 to take a 68-45 lead on the way to a 102-73 win.

In the playoffs, the Cards defeated St. Louis, but lost to Drake, a team it had defeated by 42 points only weeks earlier. The score – Drake 86, U of L 71 – wasn't even close.

Immediately after the game, Stacey announced that he had signed a three-year contract to replace the coach

Denny Crum, in the leisure-suit era.

who had just drubbed him, and the players voted against taking an NIT bid. However, Hickman overruled them – "We have a responsibility to the conference to go to the NIT," he said – and the Cards went to New York against their will. Unsurprisingly, they lost to Providence, 64-58, in the first round.

When the team returned from New York, Dromo met privately with the players before announcing that he would not return as coach. He recommended that his replacement be assistant coach Bill Olsen. However, after conducting a national search, U of L hired Denny Crum,

the brash, 34-year-old assistant who had just helped John Wooden win his fifth consecutive national title at UCLA.

A few days after the announcement, Olsen took Crum to visit Dromo, still recovering from the heart attack. They went over the talented, experienced personnel that would be returning and the promising newcomers. At the end, Crum shook hands with Dromo and said, "I appreciate that you left me the makings of a pretty good ball club."

The first 15 years of Crum's tenure always will be remembered as the golden era of U of L's time in Freedom Hall. After making it to only one Final Four in the first 33 years of the NCAA tournament, the Cards went to six from 1972 through 1986. Most importantly, they broke into the college game's most elite club, winning national championships in 1980 and 1986.

Jeff Hall, Robbie Valentine, Milt Wagner and Billy Thompson celebrate winning the 1986 NCAA Championship.

Most importantly, the Cards finally began filling Freedom Hall on a regular basis. From 1982-'83 through their final season, they perennially ranked among the nation's top five in average home attendance. Before the 1984 season, the arena underwent a major renovation that included the addition of 24 luxury suites and increased capacity from 16,600 to 18,865.

University of Louisville Sports Information

Crum barks orders while Sports Information Director Kenny Klein (right) looks on.

Crum's first team had an eight-man senior class that included Jim Price, Ron Thomas, Henry Bacon, Al Vilcheck, Larry Carter, and Mike Lawhon. After losing Crum's debut game to Florida in Gainesville, the Cards won their next 15 in a row, including a sweep of Syracuse, St. Peter's and

Fordham to win the Holiday Festival in New York's Madison Square Garden.

By the end of the season, U of L had a 23-3 record, but also a pair of losses to Memphis State that necessitated a one-game playoff in Nashville to determine which team would get the Missouri Valley Conference's automatic bid in the NCAA field. This time the Cards prevailed, 83-72, to earn a trip to Ames, Iowa, for the NCAA Midwest Regional, where they defeated Southwestern Louisiana and Kansas State to give Crum a Final Four trip on his first try.

Alas for the Cardinals, their semifinal opponent – in Los Angeles, of all places – was UCLA, Crum's alma mater and former employer. The Bruins were gunning for their sixth straight title – and eighth in nine years – with a young team led by 6-11 sophomore center Bill Walton, whom Crum had recruited in his last year as Wooden's assistant.

After good-naturedly ribbing Crum before the game, Walton torched his team for 33 points, 21 rebounds and five blocked shots in UCLA's 97-77 romp. Showing mercy on his protégé, Wooden benched Walton with five minutes remaining. Two days later, the Cards lost the consolation game to North Carolina for a final 26-5 record.

It took Crum only three years to return to the Final Four. In retrospect, the 1974-'75 season was the best ever for the basketball-crazy fans who live within a 120-mile radius of Freedom Hall. Unbeaten Indiana was the nation's No. 1 team, but close behind were Louisville and Kentucky.

This group of Cards was built around Ulysses "Junior" Bridgeman and Allen Murphy, a couple of 6-5 seniors who could play anywhere on the floor. The supporting class included Wes Cox, a talented 6-5 sophomore from Louisville Male; point guard Phillip Bond, a senior from Manual; and 6-10 freshman center Ricky Gallon.

The Cards won their first 13 before losing at Bradley, 65-59. After three more victories, Crum's team stumbled again, losing at Tulsa. But it closed the season with eight

Allen Murphy (20, bottom) teamed with bookend classmate Junior Bridgeman (10, left) to lead U of L to the 1975 Final Four.

Denny Crum makes a point to Wes Cox (41), a product of Male High School's pipeline to U of L.

more wins to finish at 24-2, win the Missouri Valley, and earn a berth in the Midwest Regional, where they ripped through Rutgers, Cincinnati, and Maryland to reach the Final Four in San Diego.

Once more, the Cards were matched against UCLA, which the previous year had failed to win the national title for the first time since 1966. On the other side of the bracket was Kentucky, which had ended Indiana's unbeaten season, 92-90, in the Mideast Regional championship game.

In what many still regard as one of the best college games ever played, the Cards led the Bruins, 65-61, with only 66 seconds remaining. But UCLA tied it on two free throws by Richard Washington and a follow shot by Marques Johnson. The Cards had the game's last shot, but senior guard Junior Bridgeman missed a jumper with 0:02 remaining to send it into overtime.

With U of L holding a 74-73 lead and only 20 seconds left in the OT, UCLA fouled U of L senior Terry Howard, who was 28 for 28 from the foul line for the season. But Howard missed the front end of the bonus and Washington rebounded for UCLA. With 0:03 remaining, Washington hit a 12-footer to send the Bruins into the championship game against Kentucky.

After the game, Wooden shocked everyone by announcing that he would retire after the championship game. It was widely assumed that Crum would succeed his mentor, but on Monday Crum announced that he was withdrawing his name from consideration. "I plan to be in Louisville for a long, long time," Crum said. That night he watched UCLA defeat UK, 92-85, to give Wooden his 10th national title in 12 years.

The Cards got off to an 18-4 start in 1975-76, but lost two of their last four regular-season games and got upset by Memphis State in the Metro Conference Tournament in Freedom Hall. That meant banishment to the NIT, where they lost to Providence in the first round.

University of Louisville Sports Information

Darrell Griffith became "Dr. Dunkenstein" at U of L.

However, the gloom was dissipated on April 20 when Male High star Darrell Griffith announced that he and teammate Bobby Turner were staying home to play for the Cards. "Before I graduate," Griffith said, "I intend to bring several NCAA championships to Louisville."

The signing of Griffith was the beginning of a decade in which Crum and assistants Bill Olsen, Wade Houston, Jerry Jones, and Bobby Dotson did arguably the finest recruiting jobs in college hoops. They virtually owned Louisville, missing only on Durand "Rudy" Macklin, who

University of Louisville Sports Information

Griffith worked to improve his ball-handling before his senior year.

All photos courtesy of University of Louisville Sports Information

became a star at LSU, and Winston Bennett, who became the first Male High star since Ralph Beard to play his college ball at Kentucky. But they got Jerry Eaves out of Ballard High, Manuel Forest out of Moore, Herb Crook out of Eastern, and Tony Kimbro out of Seneca.

They also ventured to the suburbs of New York City to get the McCray brothers, Scooter and Rodney; to Camden, New Jersey, to get Milt Wagner, Kevin Walls, and Billy Thompson; and to the rural South to pluck Derek Smith out of Hogansville, Georgia; Charles Jones out of Scooba, Mississippi; Lancaster Gordon out of Jackson, Mississippi; Wylie Brown out of Sylvester, Georgia; Pervis Ellison out of Savannah, Georgia; and Kenny Payne out of Laurel, Mississippi.

After three years, it looked as if Griffith wasn't going to fulfill his promise of bringing a national championship to Louisville. The Cards lost to UCLA (again!) in the NCAA's first round to end his freshman year, to DePaul in double OT in the second round to end his sophomore

year, and to Arkansas, again in the second round, to end his junior season.

But Griffith worked incredibly hard the summer before his senior year and was a different player when practice started. Although the Cards were dealt a severe blow early in the season when sophomore Scooter McCray was injured against Tennessee in Knoxville and declared out for the season, his "little" brother Rodney took his place in the starting lineup alongside Griffith, Derek Smith, Jerry Eaves and Wylie Brown. Amazingly, the Cards didn't miss a beat.

Led by the acrobatic Griffith and his 42-inch vertical leap, this was the team that came to be known as "The Doctors of Dunk." Before the season, after a scrimmage in Indiana, reserve Poncho Wright proclaimed that "The Ville's going to The Nap." Translated, he meant that "The Ville," as in Louisville, was going to India-nap-olis, his hometown and the scene of the 1980 Final Four.

The quote appeared in a *Courier-Journal* column, the first time Louisville had ever been known as "The Ville."

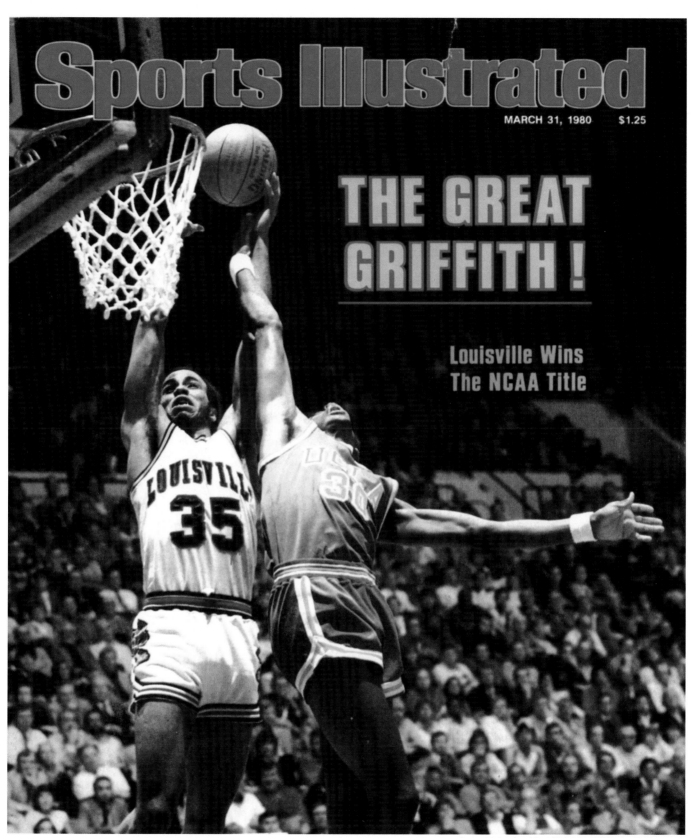

Sports Illustrated

MARCH 31, 1980 $1.25

THE GREAT
GRIFFITH !

Louisville Wins
The NCAA Title

The *Sports Illustrated* cover blurb was right on the money.

Derek Smith (43) and Billy Thompson (55) were high-flying Cards.

Coach Denny Crum and Derek Smith are interviewed by Billy Packer of CBS.

The game that set the tone for the season was a 75-65 victory over a talented Ohio State team on December 19 before a standing-room-only crowd in Freedom Hall. Something changed that night for both the team and the crowd. The atmosphere was big-league, in every respect, and it set the tone for the foreseeable future.

On the way to a 33-3 record, the Cards invented the "high five." Sophomores Derek Smith and Wylie Brown, both natives of Georgia, communicated with each other in a form of Pig Latin. Freshman Rodney McCray became known as "Hard" for the way he played and the stare he leveled at opponents.

After beating Iowa in the national semifinals in Market Square Arena, Brown managed to misplace his artificial thumb, which created a minor furor the day before the final game. But it finally was dug out of a Dumpster at the team hotel, meaning that everything was right with the Cards as they prepared to see if Griffith could fulfill the promise he had when he signed.

Co-captains Darrell Griffith and Tony Branch celebrate the 1980 NCAA Championship.

In the championship game in Indianapolis' Market Square Arena, Crum once more faced off against UCLA. But now the Wooden mystique was gone and the Bruins were coached by Larry Brown. The game turned in the second half when U of L's Jerry Eaves blocked what seemed to be a certain layup by UCLA's Kiki Vandeweghe that would have put the Cards in a deep hole. Instead, they rallied for a 59-54 win.

At a victory celebration in Freedom Hall, Kentucky Governor John Y. Brown Jr. asked the crowd, "Why are we meeting in this old building?" Picking up the cue, Crum began to lobby for either a new arena or a Freedom Hall renovation.

In 1981, the Cards bid to repeat was foiled when U.S. Reed of Arkansas hit a 49-footer at the buzzer to give the Razorbacks a 74-73 victory in the Midwest Regional. Undaunted, U of L returned to the Final Four the next two years, only to be eliminated by Georgetown in the 1982

semifinals in the Louisiana Superdome and by Houston's "Phi Slamma Jamma" team in the '83 semis in Albuquerque.

The Houston game, pitting the nation's two most athletic teams, was supposed to be for the national championship. The Cards led 57-49 in the second half, but then ran out of gas – and oxygen – in Albuquerque's high altitude. The Cougars went on a 21-1 run on the way to a 94-81 victory. Incredibly, they got beat in the finals by North Carolina State, the biggest upset in NCAA championship game history.

Milt Wagner was known as "The Ice Man" for being cool under pressure.

As Governor Brown's term neared its end in 1983 (Governors could be elected for only one four-year term in those days), the issue of a new arena for Louisville still was a political basketball bouncing endlessly between statehouse and courthouse. The issue became stalled in a sort of political four corners until Brown finally came up with a $13.5 million renovation plan.

After a brief scare early in 1984 when the new administration of Governor Martha Layne Collins threatened to table the project, the work began at the end of the basketball season, continued through the summer and was completed by November 18, when U of L held a public scrimmage to show off the finished product. The floor had been dropped ten feet, which increased the seating capacity and brought the fans closer to the floor. In addition, 24 luxury suites ringed the lower arena.

The party mood at the home opener on December 1 against Virginia Commonwealth turned somber when senior guard Milt Wagner suffered an ankle injury and hobbled off

Pervis slams one down.

Lancaster Gordon

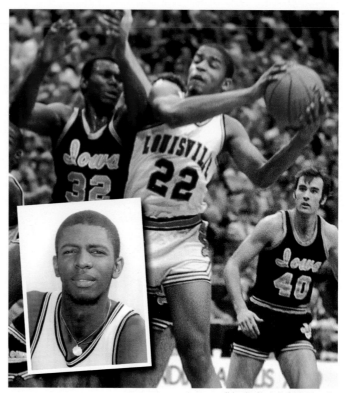

Rodney and Scooter (inset) McCray.

the floor. He was declared out for the season, which sent the Cards reeling to the NIT and a 19-18 final record, by far their worst season under Crum.

But the loss of Wagner proved to be a blessing in disguise. As a redshirt senior in 1985-'86, he was the catalyst of the team that gave Crum his second national title. In the title game against Duke, freshman Pervis "Never Nervous" Ellison put back Jeff Hall's miss for a 68-65 lead and added two free throws to put the Cards up by five with 0:27 to play. After Duke scored four straight, Wagner calmly swished two free throws with 0:02 remaining to give U of L a 72-69 win in Dallas' Reunion Arena.

Although nobody could have foreseen it at the time, U of L had reached its pinnacle under Crum. In his final 14 years, the Cards failed to return to the Final Four and began a downward slide that was almost imperceptible until the proud Cardinals dipped to 12-20 in 1997-'98.

One reason was that Wade Houston, Crum's top recruiter, went to Tennessee in 1989 and took his superstar son, Allan, who had committed to U of L, with him. Another was that for some reason, the reservoir of talent in the Louisville high school ranks dried up. Throughout the '90s, the only Louisville products who played significant roles for the Cards

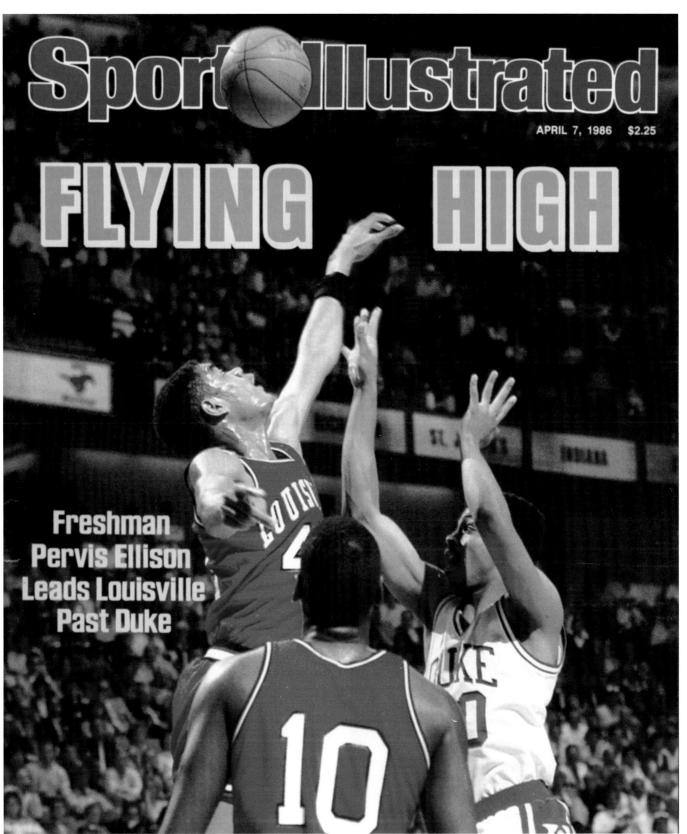

Sport Illustrated

APRIL 7, 1986 $2.25

FLYING HIGH

Freshman
Pervis Ellison
Leads Louisville
Past Duke

Ellison blocked Duke's title hopes in 1986.

University of Louisville Sports Information

Athletic Director Tom Jurich engineered U of L's move into the Big East Conference.

University of Louisville Sports Information

U of L's award-winning cheerleaders fire up the Cards crowd.

were Dwayne Morton, DeJuan Wheat, Jason Osborne and Tony Williams.

After three more seasons in which the Cards failed to win 20 games or an NCAA tournament game – they dipped to 12-19 in 2000-'01 and didn't even get an NIT bid – Crum and Athletics Director Tom Jurich worked out an agreement by which Crum would retire.

In 29 years, Crum had a 364-84 record in Freedom Hall. No wonder the floor was named in his honor.

Rick Pitino didn't take the Louisville job simply because he loved Freedom Hall, but it was a factor. As the coach at

Denny Crum addresses the crowd when the Freedom Hall floor was named in his honor.

Ex-UK coach Rick Pitino returned to the Commonwealth to coach the Cards.

Providence and Kentucky, he was 12-2 all-time in Freedom Hall and 3-1 against Louisville.

Indeed, Freedom Hall was the launching pad for his first trip to the Final Four. That came in 1986-'87, when Pitino came to Louisville for the NCAA Mideast Regional with a running, shooting, pressing bunch built around point guard Billy Donovan. The Friars stunned Alabama and Georgetown to advance to the Final Four in New Orleans, where they were eliminated by Syracuse.

After returning from the 2005 Final Four, Jim Host, then Secretary of the Commerce Cabinet for Governor Ernie Fletcher, began talking with U of L and Louisville business leaders about building a new arena in Louisville.

At first Host favored the state fairgrounds, next to Freedom Hall, as the arena site. However, the business community convinced him the arena needed to be downtown to have the

Larry O'Bannon (34) and Ellis Myles (2) helped Pitino rebuild the program.

Francisco Garcia (left) and Taquan Dean (above)
were stars in U of L's 2005 run to the Final Four in St. Louis.

maximum economic-development impact. Host left state government in the fall of 2005 and became chairman of the Louisville Arena Authority, which finally put together a deal for the arena to be built on downtown riverfront property owned by Louisville Gas & Electric.

While these plans were being formulated, the Cards dropped to 21-13 in 2005-'06, but had the distinction of setting the Freedom Hall attendance record when a crowd of 20,091 jammed in for the Connecticut game on Jan. 21, 2006. (Before the renovation in 1984, the biggest crowd was the 17,661 that saw the Cards beat Cincinnati on February 22, 1969.)

The 2006 Cards had to settle for the NIT, where they lost in the semifinals to South Carolina. But the next year they advanced to the NCAA round of 32, losing to Texas A&M in Rupp Arena, before posting glorious back-to-back seasons in which they went to the Elite Eight before losing to

Terrence Williams (left), David Padgett (4) and Earl Clark (5) always dominated the space around the rim.

North Carolina and Michigan State, respectively.

The glue of the '07 and '08 teams was 6-10 center David Padgett, a transfer from Kansas who played "point center" for the Cards and set up the offense for versatile scorers such as Earl Clark, Juan Palacios, and Terrence "T-Will" Williams.

The 2008-'09 team lost twice in Freedom Hall (to UNLV and UConn) on the way to winning both the regular-season and tournament championships in a Big East Conference that many thought was the best in history, top to bottom. They became the first U of L team to finish first in the final regular-season polls and the first to be the No. 1 overall seed in the NCAA tournament.

Their leader, the charismatic 6-6 Williams, was on the cover of *Sports Illustrated* four consecutive weeks, and

they had an excellent freshman center tandem in Samardo Samuels and Terrence Jennings. They wore out opponents with depth and defensive pressure. Although they didn't have a player as talented as, say, Oklahoma's Blaine Griffin or North Carolina's Tyler Hansbrough, they played unselfish team ball as well as anyone in the nation.

But after rolling to wins over Morehead State, Siena, and Arizona, the Cards inexplicably struggled against Michigan State in the regional final. The fact that the Final Four was scheduled for Ford Field in Detroit gave the Spartans an extra emotional incentive that helped carry them to a 62-54 victory.

The team that will represent U of L in the 2009-'10 season is a far cry from the one that moved into Freedom

In 2005, Rick Pitino became the first coach to lead three programs to the Final Four.

Hall fulltime in 1957-'58. For one thing, it's integrated. For another, it includes talent from around the nation instead of just the tight little area where Hickman and Dromo did most of their recruiting – Kentucky and its bordering states.

When Tom Jurich became U of L's athletics director, he said he wanted the Cardinals to field national-championship caliber teams in all sports, not only men's basketball. That touched off an unprecedented era of facilities-building and program-building. One of the most prominent beneficiaries of Jurich's philosophy was the women's basketball team, which had won a few titles

Sellout crowds have been routine since Freedom Hall was renovated in 1984. Above, a "whiteout" blankets the arena.

in the Metro Conference and Conference USA, but never been a factor on the national scene.

Blessedly, however, the Cards' move to the Big East Conference coincided happily with Angel McCoughtry's arrival on campus in 2005. A product of the Baltimore high school ranks, she picked the same uniform number worn by Darrell Griffith (35) and, like "Dr. Dunkenstein," took the Cards to heights they had never before scaled.

In McCoughtry's first three seasons, the Lady Cards had records of 19-10, 27-8, and 26-10. They were eliminated in the NCAA's first round her freshman season, the second round her sophomore year, and the Sweet Sixteen in her junior year of 2007-'08. You might say the public noticed. On January 12, 2008, a crowd of 19,123 jammed Freedom Hall to see the Lady Cards play UConn.

Angel's senior season was, well, heavenly.

On December 14, 2008, a crowd of 16,337 *paid* to see the Lady Cards whip up on the UK Lady Cats in Freedom Hall. That was a new state and Big East record for a paid crowd, as opposed to one in which many of the seats were giveaways. And from there, the Lady Cards soared to the greatest season a women's team from the Commonwealth has ever produced.

Although they lost to undefeated UConn 76-54 in the NCAA championship game in St. Louis, McCoughtry and her teammates accomplished the following:

- First U of L women's team, in any sport, to play in a national title game.
- First women's basketball All-American, McCoughtry, who won the honor three years.

With the help of Angel McCoughtry (left), the Lady Cards soared to new heights.

University of Louisville Sports Information

Candyce Bingham

University of Louisville Sports Information

Jeff Walz coached the Lady Cards to the 2009 NCAA title game.

- First 30-win season. The Lady Cards finished 35-5, with three of the losses to UConn.
- First Final Four team in U of L women's basketball history.
- First U of L women's team to rank in the top 10 nationally in attendance, averaging a school-record 7,111 fans per game in Freedom Hall, including two of the nation's three largest crowds during the regular season.

The Cards were coached by Jeff Walz, who grew up in Northern Kentucky. Although his dad played football at UK and a sister was a star basketball player, Jeff never figured he could accomplish much in sports because of a stuttering problem that made him shy and reluctant to express himself in public.

For her first two years at U of L, McCoughtry turned off some fans with her incessant pouting and posturing. But when Walz arrived before her junior season, he put together a tape to show her how immature she looked. She took the message to heart and toned down her attitude for the benefit of all concerned.

Even when starting center Chauntise Wright went down with a knee injury before the 2008-'09 season, the Lady Cards rallied around McCoughtry. When Angel had the rare off night, teammates such as sophomore guard Desiree Byrd and center Keisha Hines stepped up to pick up the slack.

"We're disappointed to lose," said Byrd after the title game, "but we're proud."

THE CARDINALS' HOME NEST   **147**

Cassius Clay squares off against Tunney Hunsaker in 1960.

BOXING

Perhaps the most historically important event ever held in Freedom Hall was a boxing match that drew only around 6,000 spectators. It took place on October 29, 1960, and it was the professional debut of Louisville native Cassius Clay, who was fresh off winning the light-heavyweight gold medal at the Olympic Games in Rome. His opponent was Tunney Hunsaker, the police chief of Fayetteville, West Virginia, who moonlighted as a prize fighter. The afternoon of the fight, Clay and Hunsaker met at a downtown sporting goods store. "He came in – he knew I was there – and he fooled around a little, bounced a basketball or something like that, and I could see he was nervous," Hunsaker later told biographer Thomas Hauser.

Only three days before the fight, Clay had signed a management agreement with the Louisville Sponsoring Group, a collection of 11 wealthy, young, civic-minded businessmen who agreed to put up the necessary $25,000 or so to launch Clay as a professional. The deal was fair to both sides: The sponsoring group would pay all management, training, travel and promotional expenses, in addition to setting up a trust fund for him, giving him a $10,000 signing bonus, and, for the first two years, paying him a salary of $333 per month against earnings. In exchange, they would get 50 percent of any earnings for the first two years with options to extend the contract on a yearly basis.

The group hired William H. King to promote Clay's first fight. He had put on a sport-boat-vacation show the year Freedom Hall opened, and it turned into such a bonanza that he put on similar shows in Miami, Mobile, and Oakland. Beginning in 1958, King had promoted more nationally televised boxing shows from Freedom Hall than Madison Square Garden did from New York. But then came a wave of scandals that forced sponsors to drop boxing, killing the sport as a TV attraction until the late 1970s.

Photo courtesy of Billy Reed

Billy Reed interviews William H. King.

King's plunge into boxing coincided happily with Clay's rise as an amateur fighter. Intrigued by the kid's outgoing personality and unique style, King would take him to a downtown men's store and buy him clothes whenever he won a fight. Clay didn't forget. Even after he won the world heavyweight championship, changed his name to Muhammad Ali, and became one of the most famous people on the planet, he would help King without pay whenever King needed him to promote his harness track, Louisville Downs, or other ventures.

Although Freedom Hall was far too big for Clay's first fight, King decided to go first-class because he knew the boxing world was watching closely. Unfortunately for Clay, he couldn't knock out Hunsaker and had to settle for a six-round decision.

"He was as fast as lightning," Hunsaker said years later, "and he could hit from any position without getting hit. I tried just about every trick I knew to knock him off balance, but he was just too good. After the fight, when I got home that night, Judge Abbott asked me, 'What did you think about that boy?' And I told him, 'Mr. Abbott, he'll be heavyweight champion of the world someday.' It was a real honor for me to have been in the ring with him."

The trainer in Clay's corner that night was Fred Stoner, who ran the Columbia Gym in Louisville and had worked extensively with Clay as an amateur. But the Louisville Sponsoring Group figured he needed a trainer with more professional experience and a bigger reputation. So, after sending him to California to train with the still-active veteran Archie Moore, the Sponsoring Group talked to Harry Markson, the president of Madison Square Garden, and he recommended that they talk to Angelo Dundee, who trained out of the Fifth Street Gym in Miami. Among Dundee's best fighters was Willie Pastrano, a light-heavyweight world champion.

On December 19, 1960, Ali began working with Dundee, and eight days later he scored a fourth-round knockout over Herb Siler, the first of four straight fights in Miami Beach. After knocking out Tony Esperti, Jim Robinson, and Donnie Freeman, he returned to Louisville to fight Lamar Clark on April 19, 1961.

With William H. King as the promoter again, Clay knocked out Clark in the second round to run his professional

The Courier-Journal

Wearing his Olympic trunks, Clay throws a hard right that has Lamar Clark ducking desperately.

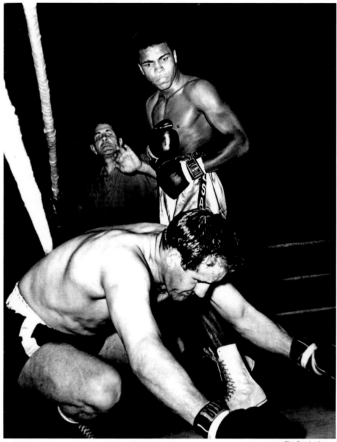

The laser-look at a fallen foe was to become an Ali trademark.

The fighter then known as Cassius Clay ducks away from an Alonzo Johnson jab.

record to 6-0 in only six months. He next went to Las Vegas to fight a big Hawaiian named Duke Sabedong on June 26. That trip was memorable not so much for Clay's ten-round decision, but for his meeting with the wrestler Gorgeous George, who had been the inspiration for the braggadocio that had earned Clay the nickname, "The Louisville Lip."

After dispatching Sabedong, Clay returned to Louisville for three consecutive fights in Freedom Hall – a ten-round decision over Alonzo Johnson on July 22, a six-round knockout of Alex Miteff on October 7, and a seven-round knockout of Willi Besmanoff on November 29. All three fights were televised nationally in a deal worked out between William H. King and Teddy Brenner, the matchmaker for Madison Square Garden Boxing.

"A couple of hours before the Miteff fight," Brenner said, "we realized that no one had brought boxing gloves. The stores were closed and it was too late to bring in gloves from someplace else. Finally, we found two pairs that where half horsehair and half foam rubber. They'd been lying around in some gym for a long time, and were hard as a rock. We thought it would help Miteff. He was a good puncher, and Clay couldn't punch. In the fifth round, it was an even fight, but Miteff figured to come on in the late rounds because he was a slow starter and a good body puncher. Then in the sixth, Clay hit him on the chin and knocked him out. Miteff had never been knocked out before. And in the dressing room afterward, he kept asking what happened."

Before the Besmanoff fight, Clay declared: "I'm embarrassed to get into the ring with this unrated duck – I'm ready for top contenders like (Floyd) Patterson and Sonny Liston. Besmanoff must fall in seven." And that's exactly what happened, mainly because Clay refused to knock out his foe until the round he predicted. The media loved it. Who ever heard of a fighter predicting the round he would knock out a foe and then actually doing it?

After the Besmanoff fight, Clay never fought in Louisville again. However, William H. King continued to promote closed-circuit telecasts of his bouts. In 1962, he was the only promoter to submit a bid for the national closed-circuit TV rights to the fight between Clay and Doug Jones in Madison Square Garden. He booked the event into 78

Trailed by the author, Ali gives then-wife Veronica a smooch during an early-morning run at his Deer Lake, Pennsylvania, camp.

theaters, including Freedom Hall, and made $128,000, a nice score in those days. Although Clay won a ten-round decision, Jones gave him all he could handle. Indeed, some observers thought Jones had earned the victory.

After shocking the boxing world by taking the title from the forbidding Sonny Liston on February 25, 1964, in Miami Beach, Clay came home in 1966 to fight a Freedom Hall exhibition against Jimmy Ellis, a boyhood friend and former sparring partner. He also was at ringside on October 27, 1966, when Ellis knocked out Ed Dembry in 2:18 of the first round. "That's good," he said to Ellis in the dressing room. "You earned a few dollars and you're not hurt…that's good."

After joining the Muslim religion and officially changing his name to Muhammad Ali, the champ was stripped of his title in 1967 after he refused to be inducted into the U.S. Army on the grounds that he was a Muslim minister and a conscientious objector to the war in Vietnam. Instead of going to jail, Ali appealed all the way to the U.S. Supreme Court, where he was vindicated in 1970 by a unanimous decision in his favor.

During Ali's absence, the title was split. The New York State Athletic Commission and five other states declared Joe Frazier to be their champion, but the rival World Boxing Association decided to hold an eight-fighter tournament to determine its champion. On December 2, 1967, Freedom Hall was the scene of a semifinal bout between Jimmy Ellis, the hometown hero, and Oscar Bonavena of Argentina. Here's how writer Mark Kram described the bout for *Sports Illustrated*:

"The fight was the first semifinal match of the World Boxing Association's heavyweight elimination tournament. It drew 3,000 people, and the vast Freedom Hall at the Kentucky Fair and Exposition Center was really just a television studio. Even so, the bout provided Ellis and Bonavena with $75,000 each and it demonstrated once again that Bonavena, who sometimes resembles a runaway beer truck, is paid more for courage than for talent…

"Last week's production was hardly memorable. Ellis, a

sort of picture fighter, did the best he could with Bonavena, a difficult opponent who has no style and does not fight from a right-handed or left-handed stance. Ellis did succeed in following his fight plan, which was not exactly what Muhammad Ali advised. Early on Saturday, Ellis picked up the phone and it was Ali on the other end saying, "We goin' to dance, baby, dance." Ellis told his old friend, for whom he once was a sparring partner, 'I'll dance, but not like you. There's more than one way to win a fight.'"

Ellis scored a 12-round decision that should have been a knockout. But much to the chagrin of Dundee, who managed Ellis as well as Ali, he kept propping up Bonavena instead of letting him fall. Kram noted that in his *Sports Illustrated* story before offering his insight into the complicated Ali-Ellis relationship.

"Dundee may have difficulty freeing Ellis from his hangup, making him believe that he is a special person and no longer the flop who fought the best middleweights during the early '60s and took unbearable punishment trying to make the weight. More than anything, though, Dundee must make Ellis believe that he is no longer the professional sparring partner, Muhammad Ali's shadow.

"The rules of a sparring partner's conduct come easily to Ellis, but they are the kind of rules that have to mark any man who has pride. Soon, the sparring partner has no identity, and he becomes a part of the scene, like the smell of wet gloves or the heavy bag. The sparring partner does not punch the light bag or skip rope while the champion is on stage. He does not interject any comment when the press is talking to the champ. He must not look for reporters but let them seek him out and, when asked a question, always remember who provides the bread and pitch for the champ. Also, he must respect the champ's privacy and position, and sit with the champ or go places with him only when asked. With Ali, Jimmy Ellis knew his place. He was the very model of a proper sparring partner…

"Though the relationship between Ali and Ellis was not strained, it did not cut deep. They were never close friends. The two men belonged to different worlds and their association really only existed because of their common boyhood in Louisville. Ali is driven by more sophisticated dreams than Ellis. For the most part, Ellis has remained untouched by the same world and social revolution that Ali embraced and then helped to make. Certainly, there is evidence to show that Ali sought to protect his friend; he ordered the Muslims to leave Ellis alone, and little or no pressure was applied to convert him to the faith. Still, Ellis was to some degree suspect by association. Ellis thought he might have to quit the Ali camp because of it."

After his decision over Bonavena, Ellis defeated Jerry Quarry in Oakland to win the WBA version of the title. He made one successful defense, against Floyd Patterson on September 4, 1968, in Stockholm, but then suffered a fourth-round knockout to Joe Frazier on February 16, 1970, in a fight that consolidated the titles. When Ali began his comeback on October 26, 1970, with a third-round knockout of Quarry in Atlanta, Ellis again faded into the background.

However, after Ali suffered his first professional loss to Frazier on March 8, 1971, in Madison Square Garden, his next fight was against Ellis on July 26 in Houston. The fight was memorable mostly because Dundee didn't work in Ali's corner for the first and only time in their association. Ellis acquitted himself well before getting knocked out in the 12th round. That was to be the last hurrah for Ellis, but the first step on the way back to the title for Ali.

In the days before cable TV, Freedom Hall often served as the scene of big closed-circuit TV fights. This sometimes required a lot of dexterity on the part of the Freedom Hall staff, as former executive director Don Johnston once related.

"We had a U of L basketball game scheduled before a closed-circuit TV fight – the second Ali-Frazier fight, I think it was," Johnston said. "Well, we had it all planned out that

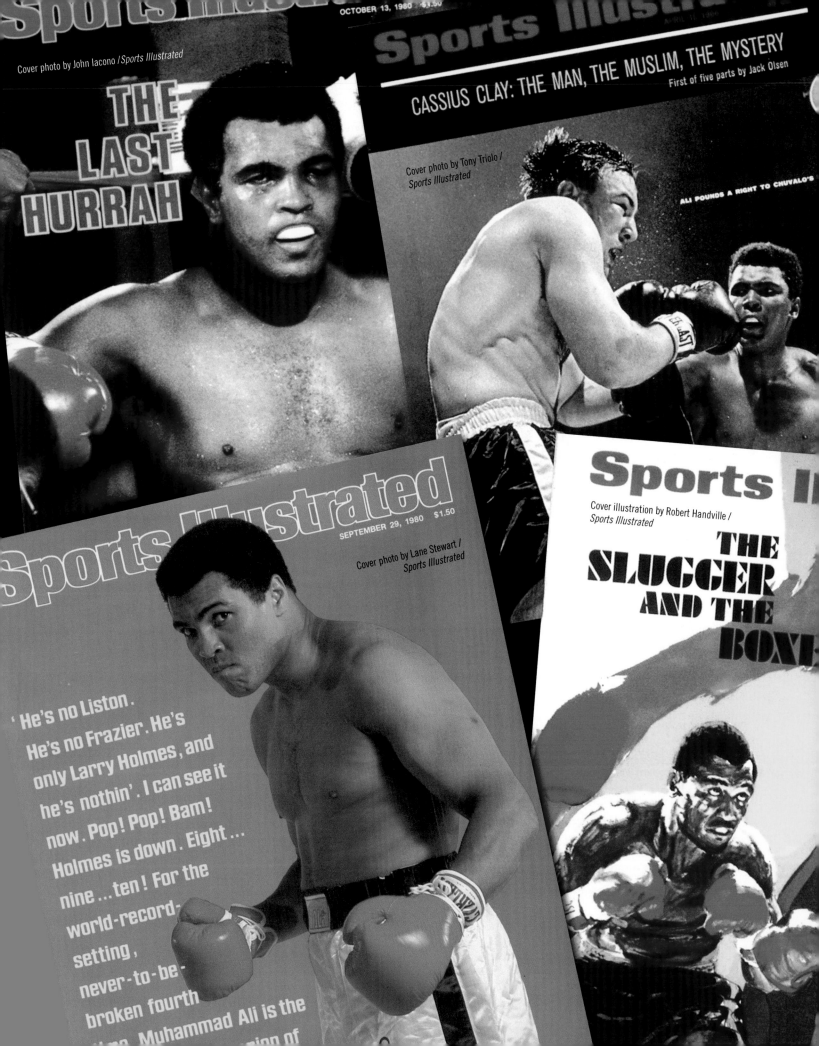

THE
LAST
HURRAH

OCTOBER 13, 1980 $1.50

Sports Illustrated

CASSIUS CLAY: THE MAN, THE MUSLIM, THE MYSTERY
First of five parts by Jack Olsen

ALI POUNDS A RIGHT TO CHUVALO'S

Sports Illustrated

SEPTEMBER 29, 1980 $1.50

'He's no Liston.
He's no Frazier. He's
only Larry Holmes, and
he's nothin'. I can see it
now. Pop! Pop! Bam!
Holmes is down. Eight...
nine...ten! For the
world-record-
setting,
never-to-be-
broken fourth
time Muhammad Ali is the

Sports

THE
SLUGGER
AND THE
BOX

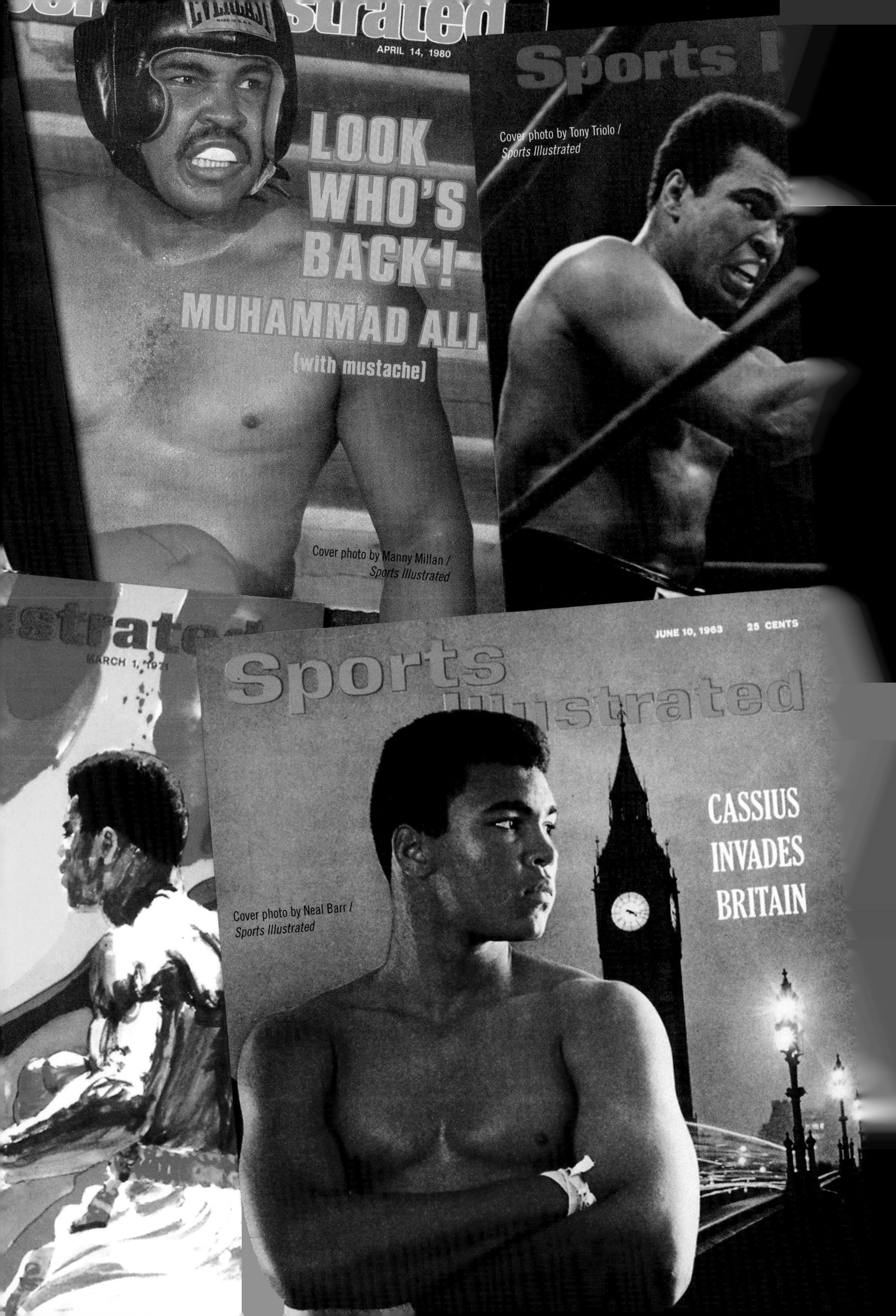

APRIL 14, 1980

LOOK WHO'S BACK!

MUHAMMAD ALI,

(with mustache)

Cover photo by Manny Millan /
Sports Illustrated

Cover photo by Tony Triolo /
Sports Illustrated

MARCH 1, 1971

Sports Illustrated

JUNE 10, 1963   25 CENTS

Cover photo by Neal Barr /
Sports Illustrated

CASSIUS INVADES BRITAIN

we could clear the basketball crowd and have just enough time to set up the cameras and TV screens and get the fight crowd in. You have to get a fight crowd in on time, because if the fight is over after 13 seconds of the first round and the people couldn't get in – well, then you've got a real problem on your hands.

"We thought we had everything worked out to the last split-second, but then the Commonwealth of Kentucky changed times on us. It was during the energy crisis and we shifted from daylight to standard. What it meant to us was that we had only 45 minutes between events instead of an hour and 45 minutes. We had all the contracts signed, so there wasn't anything we could do but plunge ahead. Fortunately, with a lot of prodding and hustling, we got the fight crowd in just in the nick of time."

It's a historical oddity that Louisville's third heavyweight championship of the last century, Greg Page, never did fight in Freedom Hall, but Mike Tyson, who achieved the status that Page never did, essentially had his career ended in Freedom Hall.

Page grew up dreaming of fighting a heavyweight title defense in Freedom Hall, something neither Ali nor Ellis ever did, but he started modestly, making his professional debut on February 16, 1979, with a second-round knockout of Don "Madman" Martin before a crowd of 7,500 in the downtown Commonwealth Convention Center, which was operated by the Kentucky State Fair Board.

Of Page's first 12 fights, five were fought in Louisville, either at the Commonwealth Convention Center or the Louisville Gardens, and one was held in Lexington's Rupp Arena. But after defeating Leroy Boone on September 12, 1980, at the Commonwealth Convention Center, Page fought in Louisville only once more – a first-round KO of David Mauney on March 24, 1989 – until he was washed up and near the end of his career.

Muhammad Ali's Kentucky Athletic Hall of Fame plaque hangs in the Freedom Hall concourse.

No less an authority than Ali anointed Page as a future champion. After sparring a round with Page in Louisville in the late 1970s, Ali declared, "That boy hit me so hard that he almost knocked me into tomorrow."

The torch seemed to be symbolically passed between the two on December 10, 1981, in Nassau, Bahamas. On the same card where Ali dropped a ten-round decision to journeyman Trevor Berbick, the last fight of his professional career, Page ran his record to 18-0 with a fourth-round knockout of Scott LeDoux.

However, after the death of his father, Albert, Page fell into the hands of the sharks. Rival promoters Don King and Butch Lewis battled each other for exclusive rights to Page, and all this did was give Page the big head.

He was overweight and out of shape on March 9, 1984, when he fought Tim Witherspoon for the vacant World Boxing Council title and he lost a 12-round mixed decision. He then got beat by David Bey on August 31, 1984, in a U.S. Boxing Association title bout, but came back on December 1 of that year to score an eighth-round knockout of Gerrie Coetzee in South Africa to claim the WBA championship.

In his first title defense, Page lost a unanimous decision to Tony Tubbs on March 29, 1985, in Buffalo. He continued fighting until 1993, took a two-year break after being knocked out by Bruce Seldon in Puerto Rico, and then began an ill-

For all intents and purposes, Danny Williams (left) ended Mike Tyson's career in Freedom Hall on July 30, 2004.

fated comeback in 1996 that culminated on March 9, 2001, when he fought a nobody named Dale Crowe for $1,500 in the parking lot of an Erlanger, Kentucky, nightclub.

Crowe knocked out Page in the tenth round and injured him so severely that he spent ten days in a coma. When he finally regained consciousness, Page was paralyzed and spent the rest of his life confined to a wheelchair. He died in 2009 of complications from those injuries, without ever fulfilling his dream of having a title defense in Freedom Hall.

During the last half of his career, Page's main claim to fame resulted from his work as a sparring partner for Tyson before Tyson's February 2, 1990 fight against James "Buster" Douglas in the Tokyo Dome. In one of their sessions, Page knocked Tyson down, the first hint that Tyson might be ripe for an upset. Sure enough, Douglas knocked out him out in

the tenth round, which might have been the heavyweight division's most shocking upset since Clay beat Liston in their first bout.

As fate would have it, Tyson brought Freedom Hall back into the national spotlight as a boxing venue when he fought unheralded Danny Williams of Great Britain on July 30, 2004. Fighting in Muhammad Ali's hometown before a big crowd that cheered his every move, Tyson tried with every punch to score the kind of spectacular knockout that would make him a heavyweight contender once again at the age of 38.

The crowd of 17,253 that nearly filled Freedom Hall came to see a knockout by Tyson, and when Tyson rocked Williams with a big uppercut and some left hooks in the first two rounds it looked like they would get what they wanted.

Big-time boxing returned to Freedom Hall in
2004. Note the absence of a smoky haze.

But Tyson was cut in the third round, and Williams showed he was going to be the bully in this fight. He hit Tyson on the break, losing a point, then hit him low, and the referee took another point.

"Every single round that went by, his punching power seemed to grow less," Williams said. "So I knew I was going to take him out."

In the fourth round, Williams landed a flurry of punches that sent Tyson sprawling into the ropes, perhaps ending his career with the same kind of fury that Tyson once unleashed on other fighters. The fighter once called the baddest man on the planet went down from a final right hand, then lay helplessly along the ropes, blood streaming down his face.

Tyson tried to get up to beat the count, then fell down again. Down for the count, Tyson could only watch the ref count him out and the fight was waved to a stunning close at 2:51 of the fourth round.

It was Tyson's first fight in 17 months, and only his second since taking a beating from former heavyweight champion Lennox Lewis two years earlier. But Lewis was a legitimate world champion, while the 31-year-old Williams' biggest claim to fame was winning the British heavyweight title.

He was desperately trying to resurrect a career that made him more than $300 million, but the loss to a 9-1 underdog perhaps signals the end of an era in the heavyweight division. "People forget this isn't a peak Mike Tyson. This was a Mike Tyson who was 38 years old," Williams said. "I thought I could win."

The loss was Tyson's first in 41 non-title fights and it dropped his career record to 50-5 with 44 KOs. Tyson earned about $8 million, but kept only $2 million of it, with the rest going to pay off some of the $38 million he owed to creditors under a bankruptcy reorganization plan.

"I'm sorry," Tyson told trainer Freddie Roach after the fight. "I'm disappointed."

"You don't have to be sorry with me," Roach replied.

On the undercard, Laila Ali, daughter of the former heavyweight champion, fought Monica Nunez in the same building where her father made his pro debut 44 years

The Courier-Journal

Another Ali, Laila, wins in Freedom Hall.

earlier. Although Muhammad Ali was not ringside to see his daughter fight, he no doubt would have been proud of his daughter's poise.

Throughout the fight, Laila Ali endured excessive holding by Nunez, who drew a one-point deduction in the second round for relentless hugging. In the fifth, Ali pounded Nunez to the body and threw the challenger to the canvas. By the eighth round, Nunez was holding so much the referee finally took a second point from her.

With the Freedom Hall crowd chanting "Ah-lee, Ah-lee," just as fight fans everywhere used to cheer her father, Laila dominated the fight before Nunez' corner threw in the towel at 42 seconds of the ninth round.

Kentucky star Chris Harrison drives on Glenn Robinson, Indiana's Mr. Basketball

THE FUTURE IS IN THE STARS

The Courier-Journal

Indiana's George McGinnis gets two of the 53 points he scored at Freedom Hall in 1969.

The highest honor a Kentucky high school player can earn is the title of "Mr. Basketball" and the right to wear the No. 1 jersey in the annual Kentucky-Indiana All-Star series. The annual two-game rivalry began in 1939 with the games being held in Butler Fieldhouse in Indianapolis and the Jefferson County Armory in Louisville.

In 1958, however, the Kentucky half of the series moved into Freedom Hall, where it was held annually through 1982.

During those 25 years, Indiana held a 16-9 advantage on the Kentucky team's home floor. The record crowd for Freedom Hall came in 1969, when 17,875 saw George McGinnis lead the Hoosiers to a 114-83 romp.

A 6-foot-9 man-child out of Indianapolis Washington High, McGinnis had scored "only" 23 in Indiana's win in Indianapolis, prompting Joe Voskuhl of Covington Catholic to say he didn't think McGinnis was as good as advertised.

Big mistake. In the Freedom Hall rematch, McGinnis ripped the Kentuckians for 53 points, a series record, while ripping 31 rebounds off the glass. "After the game," said Bob White of the Louisville *Courier-Journal*, "I was out on the floor trying to get some interviews, McGinnis came up to me and said, 'Where's Voskuhl?'" To his credit, Voskuhl congratulated McGinnis and said, "Obviously, he just had an average first game."

The epic McGinnis performance came just two years after 7-footer Jim McDaniels of Kentucky also got some redemption in Freedom Hall. After scoring only seven points in Kentucky's 76-67 victory in Indianapolis, McDaniels dropped 41 on the Hoosiers in Freedom Hall. Unfortunately, it wasn't enough to keep Kentucky from losing, 78-76.

Future IU star Mike Woodsen (5) beats future U of L hero Darrell Griffith in 1976.

The last big Kentucky-Indiana All-Star crowd in Freedom Hall came in 1976, when 15,780 showed up to see Male High's brilliant Darrell Griffith lead the Kentucky squad. The 6-3 Griffith was such a prodigious leaper that he already was being compared with Julius "Doctor J" Erving, whose spectacular dunks had helped the ABA reach parity with the NBA.

Although Griffith didn't disappoint, scoring 26 points and grabbing 11 rebounds, the home team lost, 96-88. The Hoosiers were led by Indiana University signee Mike Woodson, who matched Griffith's 26 points.

After that year, the game suffered a sudden drop in popularity, drawing only 9,000 in 1977 and 7,000 a year later. Nobody knew exactly why, although one theory was that fans were growing more interested in the proliferation of all-star games – such as the Kentucky Derby Festival Classic – that featured stars from around the nation instead of just Kentucky and Indiana.

In 1973, the first Derby Festival Classic featured a duel between Male High's Wes Cox, who was bound for Louisville, and 7-0 Richard Washington, who was headed for UCLA. As fate would have it, they would meet again when their respective college teams,

Reprinted with permission from *The Lexington Herald-Leader*

U of L and UCLA, squared off in the 1975 Final Four in San Diego.

As the years wore on and recruiting moved from a regional to a national phenomenon, interest slipped so badly in the Kentucky-Indiana series that the game's sponsors decided to try new venues. In 1980, the Indiana game

The Courier-Journal
Allan Houston fires a jumper in 1988.

again search for a new home. Sadly, the game that had once packed Freedom Hall became an orphan, moving from the Convention Center in Frankfort, to Diddle Arena in Bowling Green to Knights Hall at Bellarmine College in 2009.

Meanwhile, the national all-star games sponsored by McDonald's, the shoe companies and other national corporations thrived. The Derby Festival Classic maintained its place in the all-star rotation and flourished especially in years when UK, U of L and/or IU landed some of the nation's top recruits.

Over its 36 years in Freedom Hall, the Derby Festival All-Star Classic has raised more than $800,000 for such charities as the Ronald McDonald House, Kosair Charities and the Crusade for Children. Its best year was 1987, when a crowd of 19,041 set a national record for a high-school all star game. That year the game also generated more than $87,000 for the Ronald McDonald House.

Since 2005, the game's title sponsor has been adidas, which is the official equipment company for U of L, IU, Notre Dame, and many other prominent institutions.

Among the various all-star games around the nation, the competition for the highest-profile recruits is intense. Nevertheless, due at least partly to the magic name of Freedom Hall, the Derby Festival Classic has more than held its own as a marquee attraction.

Here are a few of the Derby Festival participants:

1970s – Moses Malone, Jack Givens, Rick Robey, Antoine Carr, Clark Kellogg, John Paxson, Steve Stipanovich, Kyle Macy, Darrell Griffith, Dominique Wilkins, Bill Cartwright, Sam Bowie, Isiah Thomas.

1980s – Glenn "Doc" Rivers, Len Bias, Chucky Brown, Billy King, Sam Perkins, Pervis Ellison, Matt Doherty, Milt Wagner, Chris Mullin, Bill Wennington, Felton Spencer, Rumeal Robinson, Kevin Pritchard, Rex Chapman, Rick Fox, Travis Ford, Lawrence Funderburke, Allan Houston, Tracy Murray.

was moved from Hinkle (formerly Butler) Fieldhouse to the new Market Square Arena. Then, after the 1982 game in Freedom Hall drew only 7,500 or so, the sponsoring Kentucky Lions Club decided to try Lexington's Rupp Arena for three years.

However, when the anticipated attendance boost didn't materialize, the sponsors moved it back to Freedom Hall in 1986 and received a lot of encouragement when 12,683 turned out to see Rex Chapman follow a 34-point outburst in Indianapolis with a 17-point effort that helped Kentucky to a 104-99 victory.

But attendance dropped to 8,384 in 1987 and stayed in that range for the next few years, leading the sponsors to

Richie Farmer playing 'D' on James Brewer in 1988 McDonalds game.

1990s – Damon Bailey, Eric Montross, Anfernee Hardaway, Jamal Mashburn, Damon Stoudemire, Derek Anderson, Brad Miller, Scott Padgett, Samaki Walker, Bryce Drew, Jahidi White, Nazr Mohammed, Jamaal Magloire, Michael Bradley, Ricky Davis, Larry Hughes, Quentin Richardson, Casey Jacobsen, Jamal Crawford, Samuel Dalembert, Joe Johnson, Marcus Haislip.

2000s – Darius Miles, Zach Randolph, Jared Jeffries, Dajuan Wagner, Francisco Garcia, Kirk Hinrich, Chuck Hayes, Kyle Lowry, Luke Ridnour, Marcus Williams, Ike Diogu, Kelenna Azubuike.

In the 2009 renewal, IU signees Christian Watford and Maurice Cheeks combined to score 47 points for the Gold team in a 151-145 win over the Black before

a crowd of 13,111 in Freedom Hall. During the player introductions, as UK and U of L fans cheered their own signees and booed those headed for rival schools, Cheek drew the loudest boos by waving a crimson IU flag as he bounced onto the court.

"I went and bought it and waved it around the mall a little bit," he said. "Got booed a little bit there, too."

Still, to the hardcore hoops fans in Kentucky and southern Indiana, the national games never generated as much excitement as the Kentucky-Indiana All-Star Game in its heyday, the 1950s, '60s, and '70s.

The site in Indianapolis, Hinkle Fieldhouse, was a Hoosier shrine long before the classic movie *Hoosiers* was filmed there. And the site in Louisville, Freedom Hall, was an almost instant monument when it opened in 1956. The talent that has appeared on those two floors is staggering.

Consider, if you will, an all-time Indiana all-star team that consists of George McGinnis and Larry Bird at the forwards, Kent Benson at center, and Oscar Robertson at guard with Rick Mount. Bird, from Spring Valley High in French Lick, and Robertson, from Indianapolis Attucks, quite likely would make almost anybody's all-time NBA team.

It's a measure of Robertson's greatness that even today, only Michael Jordan has matched him in all-around excellence. The difference between the two is that Jordan played in the ESPN age, where every dunk and dribble is documented, while Robertson played many games where there was no camera around to record his artistry. Still, the Big O virtually *averaged* a triple-double for his college and pro careers.

The all-time Kentucky all-star team might have Jim McDaniels and Jack Givens at forward, Wes Unseld at center, and Darrell Griffith and Rex Chapman at the guards. Both Griffith and Chapman had other-worldly leaping ability to go with unlimited range on their jump shots. Still, Unseld would be the team's foundation, just as he was on every team that was fortunate to have him.

Although Unseld was short for a center (6-foot-7) and wasn't much of a jumper, he compensated with intelligence and fundamentals. He was so massive that when he set a pick or got position under the boards, nobody could move him. And once he latched onto a rebound, he started the fast break with outlet passes that looked as if they were fired from a bazooka.

Although interest in the Kentucky-Indiana game has waned due to TV and competition from the national games, earning the No. 1 jersey still means something in both states. In the early 2000s, the former players who had earned the "Mr. Basketball" designation in Kentucky even started a club – one of the most exclusive ones to be found anywhere.

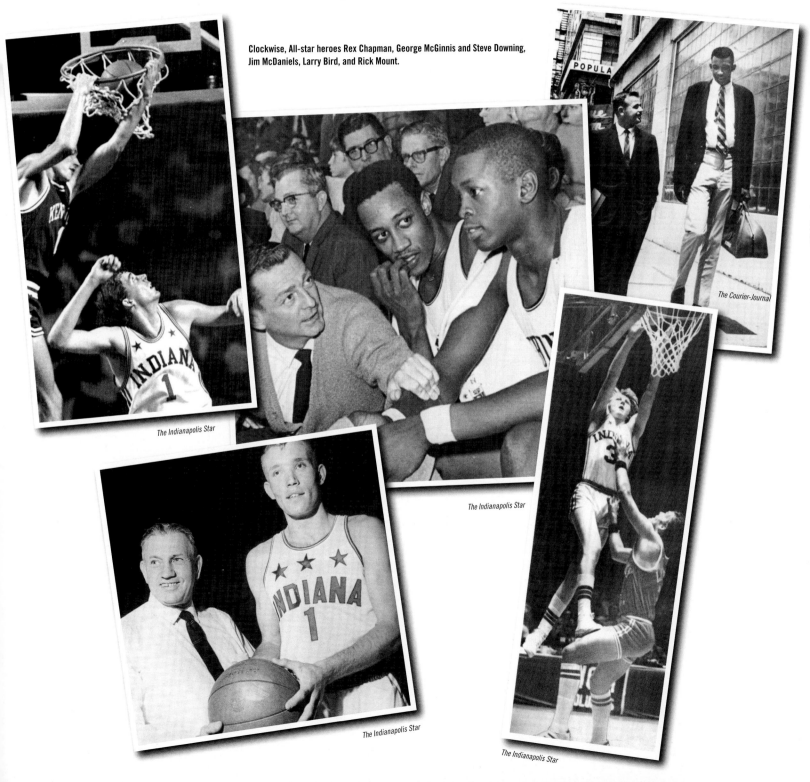

Clockwise, All-star heroes Rex Chapman, George McGinnis and Steve Downing, Jim McDaniels, Larry Bird, and Rick Mount.

The Indianapolis Star

The Courier-Journal

The Indianapolis Star

The Indianapolis Star

The Indianapolis Star

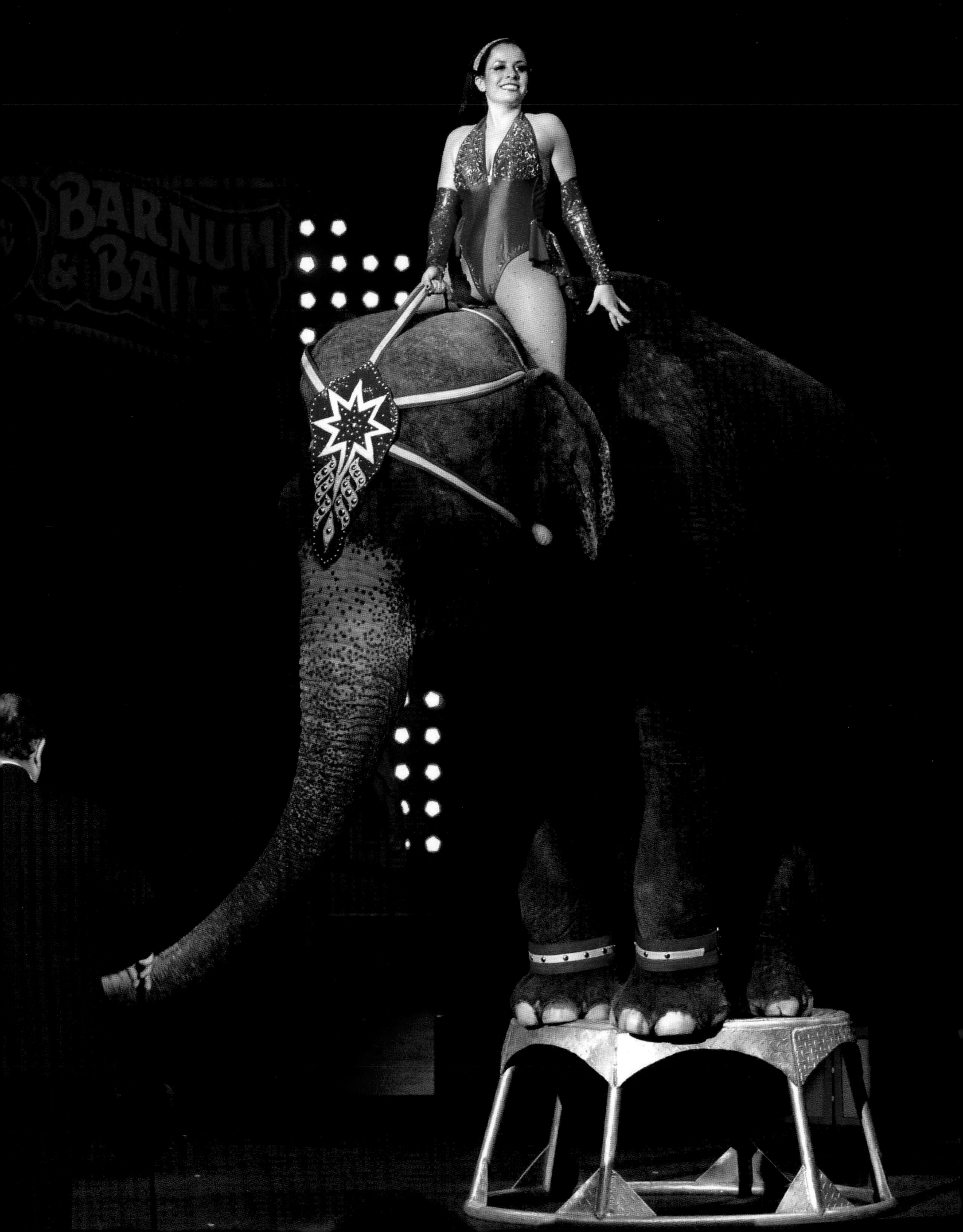
BARNUM

FAMILY ENTERTAINMENT

Although basketball is what earned Freedom Hall iconic status in the sports world, the arena also has been the scene of countless ice shows, circuses, concerts, rodeos, horse shows, and tractor pulls. It has been a place of escape – a safe place where children of all ages could go to forget their problems, lose themselves in their imaginations, and allow themselves to be entertained for a few hours.

Fortunately, the only time the arena was hit by a natural disaster, nothing of significance was going on in or around the building. That was just before 5 p.m. on April 3, 1974, when a killer tornado ripped off most of the East Wing's roof, twisted some light poles in the parking lot, and flattened most of the horse barns.

Family entertainment always has been the cornerstone of the Fair Board's philosophy and Freedom Hall's identity. So at one time or another, the arena has been circus big top, ice show center stage, and vaudeville theater for clowns of all sorts.

Harlem Globetrotters: When the act appeared in Freedom Hall on January 18, 2009, it was more than 80 years old, the last vestige of vaudeville on the American entertainment scene. But the magic of Reece "Goose" Tatum and Marques Haynes and Nat "Sweetwater" Clifton was still

The Harlem Globetrotters are frequent visitors to Freedom Hall.

Even in the home of U of L's "Doctors of Dunk," this stunt was unique.

there, real as ever, when the announcer said, "And now, ladies and gentlemen, welcome the Harlem Globetrotters and their world-famous circle routine!"

Then, while Brother Bones' famous whistling version of "Sweet Georgia Brown" played over the public-address system, the Globies, the clown princes of basketball, stood at midcourt and did those wondrous things that have delighted audiences from New York to Paris to Tokyo – passing a basketball behind their backs, twirling it on their fingers, rolling it down their backs, moving it around so fast that it's almost impossible to follow.

From their first game at Hinckley, Illinois, on January 7, 1927 through wherever they performed last night, the Globetrotters have kept the world laughing at the wacky things they do on a basketball floor. Never mind that the gags and routines are so old as to have cobwebs on them, or that the slapstick humor evokes images of silent movies.

The Globetrotters are proud, talented men who have been cited by U.S. presidents, princes, kings, dictators, popes and lots of common folks for the goodwill they have spread throughout the world. Over the years, the Globies have played more than 15,000 games in 94 countries on six continents. Once, they played for the French Foreign Legion in the Sahara Desert.

This is a play that Denny Crum never used in Freedom Hall.

The brainstorm of a canny promoter named Abe Saperstein, the Globetrotters began as a $75-a-night barnstorming troupe into an international conglomerate. In the 1970s, their popularity among kids grew enormously due to a network TV show. Or, as one kid said to Meadowlark Lemon, "You look just like you do on the cartoons."

All kidding aside, the Globetrotters are legitimate players. After leaving Kansas University after his junior season in 1959, Wilt Chamberlain played with the Globetrotters for a year before joining the NBA. Their roster also has included such big basketball names as Connie Hawkins, Bobby Joe Mason, and David "Big Daddy D" Lattin. The last starred for the 1966 Texas Western team that defeated UK's "Rupp's Runts" in the NCAA title game.

Whenever the Globetrotters stopped in Freedom Hall, which was virtually every year, it was a special homecoming for the players who were either from Kentucky or played their college ball in the Commonwealth. One of them was Dallas Thornton, an All-Stater at Louisville Male High in the early 1960s and a small-college All-American at Kentucky Wesleyan College. He became a Globetrotter in 1969, when he left the American Basketball Association, and traveled the world with the team until the late '70s.

"The pay's not as good as the pros," said Thornton in a 1975 interview, "but we got more security. Besides, it's fun. I like to play ball and make people happy. Usually, it's about 65 per cent serious and about 35 per cent clowning. But sometimes we cut down on the clowning if the guys really get into a game."

The enduring charm of the Globetrotters is that they transcend the age and race barriers. In a world that's constantly changing, they are a Rock of Gibraltar on the side of family entertainment. About the naughtiest thing that has ever happened at a Globetrotters game is when one of the clown princes yells at a mother leading a fidgety son toward the restroom, "Hey, where are you goin', lady? When you gotta go, you gotta go, right?"

Hockey and ice shows: The Freedom Hall basketball floor often has been taken up and replaced with an ice rink. The ice was broken, so to speak, in 1957 by John Harris's "Ice Capades," a touring company with a cast of 125 starring in 10 lavish productions staged over 2 ½ hours. Over the coming decades, Freedom Hall was the scene of many ice shows that featured Olympic stars.

Grace, beauty and athleticism characterize Kristi Yamaguchi and the ice shows held in Freedom Hall.

Freedom Hall provided a big-league venue for ice hockey, but the sport never caught on.

The ice rink in Freedom Hall gave hockey a chance to make it in Louisville, but the sport never caught on. In the late 1950s, an International Hockey League team named the Louisville Rebels played one season in Freedom Hall before moving to the smaller Armory, where they folded two years later.

In February, 1961, a crowd of 3,134 showed up in Freedom Hall to watch an exhibition between the Toledo Mercurys and the Fort Wayne Komets, after which the Komets' general manager said the facilities were as "good as you'll find in the world." Only eight months later, however, only 1,100 attended a game between the Komets and the Indianapolis Chiefs.

Finally, the Fair Board announced in July, 1985, that it was selling its outdated and little-used rink. The newly renovated Freedom Hall didn't accommodate it, and the ice shows had evolved to where they carried their rinks with them.

Rodeos and circuses: Even today, the rodeo remains as primitive as a brawl in a frontier saloon. Its main attractions – bareback riding, calf-roping, barrel-racing, saddle-bronc riding, steer-wrestling, and bronc-riding – have been unchanged since the West was won.

Even the entertainment between events is gut stuff – clowns, slapstick, a casino stage coach, trick riding, and cowgirls with bouffant hairdos, sequined tights and go-go boots. But the rodeo crowd loves it. They laugh and stomp their feet and whistle up a storm. A good ride draws thunderous applause, a poor one groans of disappointment.

Monster Truck competitions are always a fan favorite at Freedom Hall.

One of the many live WWE events televised from Freedom Hall.

Freedom Hall miraculously transformed into a dirt-bike competition track.

Arabian horses line up for judging.

Competitors line up for a trampoline and tumbling event in Freedom Hall.

Trade shows do a brisk business.

Future Farmers of America take a break on Freedom Hall's front lawn during an FFA convention.

"Mama, don't let your babies grow up to be cowboys," sang Willie Nelson

The show-biz cowgirls not withstanding, the rodeo always has been a man's game. Tough men with skin the color and texture of cowhide, with eyes tightened up from too much squinting into the sun, with hard, flat stomachs, bowed legs and grips that could easily turn a city slicker's hand into pulp.

The cowboys, the real cowboys, leave the fancy costumes to entertainers like Roy Rogers, the "singing cowboy" of Hollywood fame. Instead of gaudy shirts with sequins and fringe, they dress simply – straw Western hats, long-sleeved dress shirts, belts with huge buckles, tight jeans and, of course, cowboy boots.

Although only the biggest rodeo stars make big money, the sport is not without its rewards, one of the main ones being the satisfaction of doing exactly what you've wanted to do ever since you were big enough to turn a 27-foot rope into a lariat.

"Out here," a rodeo cowboy named Kenneth Kelley once said at Freedom Hall, "if ya don't win, ya gotta go home. Nobody pays your way. There's no guarantees."

There's more security with the rodeo's first cousin, the circus. The performers draw salaries to walk tightropes, snap their whips at tamed wild animals, juggle as they ride unicycles and do other circus stuff.

Like the rodeo, clowns are a circus staple and just about every clown worth his or her rubber nose has appeared in Freedom Hall or next door at Fairground Stadium: Presto, Buttons, and Emmett Kelly Jr., who revived the clown character, "Weary Willie," that his father had originated in 1933.

The Radio City Christmas Spectacular starring the world-famous Rockettes delighted an enthusiastic crowd in Freedom Hall on December 8, 2009. The audience was enchanted with their eye-high kicks and precision dance moves. Believers of all ages took part in a magical sleigh ride to Santa's North Pole workshop with thrilling dance numbers including the ever-popular "Parade of Wooden Soldiers," a high-energy interpretation of "The 12 Days of Christmas," and the breath-taking finale, "Let Christmas Shine."

UK - U of L SERIES

Somewhere around the end of World War II, University of Kentucky coach Adolph Rupp instituted an unofficial policy against scheduling regular-season games against other teams within the state. His argument was that if he played one state team, he would have to play them all. But what he really was saying that his program was a cut or two above its in-state rivals, so why jeopardize that border-to-border pre-eminence by risking a loss to Western Kentucky's Ed Diddle, Louisville's Peck Hickman, or his former assistant, Eastern Kentucky's Paul McBrayer?

The Courier-Journal
Adolph Rupp (left) congratulates U of L coach Peck Hickman after the Cards' 1959 win.

Although the other schools resented Rupp's imperious attitude, nobody seriously challenged him until Denny Crum took the Louisville job in 1971. The cocky young Crum came from John Wooden's side at UCLA, which had won five straight NCAA titles and seven of the previous eight. As far as he was concerned, Kentucky no longer was the top program in the state, much less all of college basketball, so why shouldn't the Wildcats play the Cardinals in the regular season?

Bill Straus
Denny Crum pushed for a series with UK from his first day on campus.

If this endeared Crum to many of U of L's fans -- and it did -- it made him Public Enemy No. 1 in Lexington. He turned up the heat after the Cardinals made the 1972 Final Four and Rupp's last team got beat in the Mideast Regional. It became a national topic in 1975, when both U of L and Joe B. Hall's third UK team made the Final Four in San Diego. (Both lost to Wooden's final UCLA team, U of L in the semifinals and UK in the championship game).

Finally, after the Cards won their first NCAA title in 1980, Crum didn't have to talk it up anymore because the media and the public were doing it for him.

In the summer of 1982, a fairly amazing crowd of 14,500 gathered in Freedom Hall to see "The Great Kentucky Shootout," a battle of alumni teams from UK and U of L that was held for the benefit of Multiple Sclerosis. It was rumored before the game that somebody from the UK athletic department had called a few former Wildcats to

Poster produced by Converse
After UK and U of L began their regular-season series, Converse put out this promotional poster.

UK - U of L SERIES   177

Joe B. Hall didn't like Freedom Hall as a "Visitor."

discourage them from playing but, said ex-Wildcat Reggie Warford, "I think you're on a very touchy subject – that's a rumor and I'll leave it a rumor."

The U of L alums won, 121-103, but nobody cared about the score. It was enough to again have the opportunity to ponder such marvels as Louie Dampier's jumper, James Lee's power dunking, Dan Issel's pump-fake, and Junior Bridgeman's smoothness.

"I don't know if it proved anything," said U of L's Rick Wilson. "We had fun and it was for a good cause. A regular-season game between us and UK ought to be a must. The crowd was great. Imagine what a regular-season game would be like."

The more Hall tried to defend Rupp's policies, the more he got ridiculed. Fans around the nation began pulling for a UK-U of L game in the NCAA tournament. It looked as if it might happen in the 1982 Mideast Regional, but the Cats spoiled it by getting upset by lowly Middle Tennessee. Finally, however, the stars aligned and the so-called "Dream Game" took place in the finals of the Mideast Regional in Knoxville, Tennessee.

After the Cards won a classic, 80-68 in overtime, Hall and UK Athletics Director Cliff Hagan remained unmoved about scheduling a regular-season series. But they were overruled by Dr. Otis Singletary, UK's president, and the university

athletics board, which ordered Hagan to begin negotiations with U of L. Singletary and the board understood what Hall and Hagan refused to admit – namely, that UK was getting pummeled in the public-relations battle.

In the summer of 1983, Hagan and U of L Athletics Director Bill Olsen jointly announced that the teams would begin a four-game series that November. The games would alternate between Lexington's Rupp Arena and Louisville's Freedom Hall, with the first one to be played in Lexington. After UK trounced U of L 65-44, writer Curry Kirkpatrick of *Sports Illustrated* taunted U of L in his lead:

Well, Louisville, as Art Baker used to say on television, you asked for it. You wanted this regular-season game with Kentucky, shouted for it, pleaded, demanded that it take place not just every sixth game or so but once every year. Now that you've gone down Interstate 64 to open the season against the boys from the big State U., now that you've finally played the game you wanted

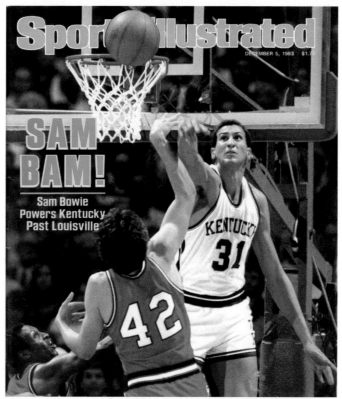

The beginning of the UK - U of L series drew attention from the national media.

so badly, how does it feel? You happy? Satisfied? Fulfilled? What about it, Cardinals? …Hey, Louisville, you still alive?

At the end of that season, doggone if the Cards didn't have to play the Cats again in Rupp Arena, this time in the semifinals of the NCAA Mideast Regional. Since the opener, the Cards had closed the gap between the two. With 0:13 to play and the Cats clinging to a 69-65 lead, Kentucky's Winston Bennett, a product of Louisville Male High, made a sensational falling-down follow of a missed Jim Master free throw. Fouled on the play, Bennett canned the free throw for a 72-65 Wildcat lead. After dispatching the Cards, UK defeated Illinois to advance to the Final Four in Seattle.

The first Freedom Hall game between the Cats and the Cards came on December 15, 1984. It was the third meeting in slightly more than one calendar year for the teams that hadn't played once in 25 years, and it turned out to be a doozie that thrilled the packed house in renovated Freedom Hall. Although U of L was playing without guard

Milt Wagner, who had suffered a season-ending knee injury against Virginia Commonwealth on December 1, the Cards withstood a sensational performance by UK's Kenny "Sky" Walter – 32 points and 15 rebounds – for a 71-64 victory. The winners were led by junior forward Billy Thompson, whose 17 points and 12 rebounds were tantalizing evidence of his potential.

"There used to be a lot of hatred," Crum said, "but I don't feel that now that we're playing. There's not as much hatred or animosity.

When the game returned to Freedom Hall on December 27, 1986, Eddie Sutton had replaced Hall as UK's coach and the Cards, coming off their second NCAA title, were heavily favored to win. However, with freshman sensation Rex Chapman knocking down six three-pointers (this was the first season of the three-point shot in college hoops) and scoring 26 points, the Cats danced off the floor with a shocking 86-51 victory. Wildcat fans were so excited about Chapman's performance that when UK returned to

Photos courtesy of Bill Straus
UK's Kenny Walker (34) battles U of L's Billy Thompson (55)

Freedom Hall for a December 30 game against Georgia, more than 16,000 showed up to watch the Wildcats' game-day shoot-around.

Rex Chapman burned the Cards for 26 points as a freshman.

Here's what *Sports Illustrated*'s Kirkpatrick said about Chapman's game against the Cards:

"Poor Louisville, at home and already struggling pitifully (now 4-6) in defense of its national championship. The Cardinals should have been forewarned by a pair of

26-point marquee performances that Chapman dished out against Boston University and Indiana. Moreover, having recruited him heavily – it is said that Chapman, last year's Mr. Basketball in Kentucky for Apollo High in Owensboro, would have enrolled at The 'Ville had Joe B. Hall remained as coach at the state university – Louisville's Denny Crum must have been aware of the precocious kid's skill and savvy.

"But this? Jerry West throwing in textbook-form three-point bombs practically without looking? (Once Chapman let loose from five-point territory.) Larry Bird half-court bounce-passing on the break? Michael Jordan hotdog dunking and fake-and-pullback dribbling over and around his taller elders? Oscar Robertson absolutely controlling the contest? Not even Kentucky coach Eddie Sutton envisioned such singular domination from one so young. 'I didn't think he could do it this soon,' said Sutton. 'He's unbelievable.'

"Seldom has an athlete merged a persona with a moment and created their own sheer magic – Joe Namath and the Super Bowl, Billie Jean King and Sex Tennis come to mind – as Chapman seems to have done with the three-point shot. If he had arrived last year, he would be just another fabulous phenom. This way, he's seriously approaching manger material. On Saturday in Freedom Hall, the son of Wayne Chapman, an ex-ABA journeyman who is the coach at Kentucky Wesleyan, made five of eight attempts from the half-moon line, and, with an insouciance bordering on disdain, looked as if he wished he could fire off 80 more. In his national TV debut, at that."

To the surprise of nobody except maybe Hall and Hagan, the series was such a big hit both locally and nationally that the original four-year contract was renewed again and again. Interestingly, the reality of the rivalry seemed to dissipate a lot of the ugly animosity that existed when UK refused to play. The fans of both teams came to look forward to the game and argue about it the year-round. And UK learned that it was possible to lose to U of L without losing an iota of

U of L's Pervis Ellison (42) and Cornelius Holden (30) outbattle UK's Reggie Hanson (35) for a rebound.

its border-to-border support.

When the teams met in Freedom Hall on New Year's Eve, 1988, Sutton was on his way to being fired as the result of a major recruiting scandal, and the Wildcat roster had been depleted by Chapman's defection to the NBA. As a result, Pervis Ellison's senior team hung a 97-75 whipping on the Cats, who were on the way to a 13-19 record, UK's first losing season since 1926-'27.

The fourth UK-U of L game in Freedom Hall took place on Dec. 29, 1990. In only his second season in Lexington, Rick Pitino had Kentucky ranked No. 18 in the nation heading into the game. The Cats' 93-85 victory was the beginning of an ugly stretch for the Cards, who lost six in a row and 11 of their next 13 on the way to a 14-16 record that ended U of L's 46-year streak of winning seasons.

On December 12, 1992, UK was ranked No. 3 nationally when it played the Cards in Freedom Hall. The Cats' 88-68 victory made Pitino 3-1 against Crum and 2-0 against U of L in Freedom Hall. The Cards had no answer for UK's 6-foot-8 Jamal Mashburn, who hit five three-pointers on the way to a game-high 27 points. Rodrick Rhodes added 20 for the winners.

This was the *Sports Illustrated* report:

"Since the schools began this regular-season series in 1983, a series for which Crum had lobbied relentlessly upon his arrival from UCLA in '71, the record is Cats 7, Cards 3. Even worse from Louisville's point of view, the teams have

University of Louisville Sports Information

U of L's DeJuan Wheat soars for a perfect layup.

traded places in terms of image and style. In the 1980s, when Crum won two NCAA titles and made two other Final Four appearances, Louisville was one of the few top teams in the country that played up-tempo ball, relying on a withering fast break and a full-court press. The Cardinals were the self-styled 'Doctors of Dunk,' remember?

"Kentucky, on the other hand, played the physical, boring, ball-control style that was in vogue at the time. The Cards had thoroughbreds, the Cats had Clydesdales. But when the 45-second shot clock was adopted for the 1985-'86 season and the three-point shot was brought in a year later, Crum reacted sluggishly to the possibilities offered by the changes, though his teams didn't begin to suffer in

University of Louisville Sports Information

Crum's teams lost their swagger after Rick Pitino took over at UK.

comparison with Kentucky until 1989-'90, when Pitino replaced Sutton in Lexington…The Wildcats have become the loose, with-it program of the 1990s while Crum's team has come to look dated, irrelevant."

But on New Year's Day, 1995, the Cards ended a four-game losing streak to the Cats and gave Crum his first win over Pitino in Freedom Hall, squeezing out an 88-86 victory built around 6-6 freshman Sophomore Samaki Walker's triple-double – 14 points, 10 rebounds, and a school-record 11 blocks. DeJuan Wheat led the Cards with 23. Walker's performance meant about as much to U of L fans as Chapman's 1986 coming-out party meant to UK diehards.

Pitino's final appearance in the series as UK coach came on New Year's Eve, 1996, when he coached the Cats to a 74-54 victory. Louisville native Derek Anderson scored UK's first seven points on three spectacular dunks and a free throw. Nevertheless, UK trailed, 28-27, at halftime. But the Cats, trailing by three heading into the final 10 minutes, went on a 35-12 run that was led by Anderson and Ron Mercer. Anderson led UK with 19 and another Louisville native, Scott Padgett, also had a nice homecoming, scoring what was then a career-high 15 to go with six rebounds.

On December 26, 1998, Tubby Smith became the fourth UK coach to match wits with Crum in Freedom Hall. The previous season, Smith's first as Pitino's successor, the Wildcats had won their second NCAA title in three years. The Cards had beaten the national title team, 79-76, in Rupp Arena, and this time they won, 83-74, to give Crum a 2-0 edge over Smith.

"Everybody thought that last year was a fluke and it probably was," Crum said. "I told our players before the game that this was the same as playing anybody else, except both teams are going to play a little harder. That's the nature of a rivalry."

Whenever the Cards looked shaky, the crowd of 20,051 lifted and carried them to a new level. And make no mistake:

University of Louisville Sports Information

The series was so intense that Crum changed his tune and tried to downplay it.

This was no fluke. The Cards seemed to get almost every loose ball or errant rebound. Simply put, they wanted it more than the passive Mildcats. In fact, UK's most aggressive moment came after the game had been decided.

With less than ten seconds remaining, U of L's Nate Johnson took a pass on the wing. The path to the hoop was as wide open as a lane on the Watterson Expressway at midnight on Christmas Eve. Johnson could have done the sporting thing and backed it out. But in a game so important and so emotionally charged, he wanted to put an exclamation point to the Cards' most important win since the previous season's upset in Rupp Arena.

So there he came, going in for a slam that might make the highlights on ESPN's SportsCenter. But Jamaal Magloire, UK's rogue of a backup center, was having none of it. He stuffed Johnson, after which the two exchanged insults and the benches emptied. Some pushing and shoving ensued, one of the few times in series history that tempers threatened to get out of control. "It (Magloire's block) was unnecessary," said Johnson. "The game was over. It was a dirty play." Because the UK locker room was closed, Magloire didn't get a rebuttal opportunity.

On January 2, 2001, in what was to be Crum's last game against UK, guard Reece Gaines delighted a Freedom Hall crowd of 20,061 by scoring six points in the first four minutes the Cards got off to a 14-4 lead. But UK led by two at halftime and pushed it to 12 in the second half. Instead of giving up, the Cards fought back and tied it inside the final minute on back-to-back threes by Gaines. UK's Tayshaun Prince made a pair of free throws with 26 seconds to go for what was to be the final margin. The Cards had two chances to win, but missed a three and turned it over on an inbounds play.

University of Louisville Sports Information

Pitino became the first—and still the only—coach to work for both sides.

After the season, Crum retired with a 675-295 record that included a 7-13 record against UK. In Freedom Hall, Crum was 4-5 against the Cats.

When the series returned to Freedom Hall on December 28, 2002, Pitino was in his second year as the Cards coach and Smith, his successor at UK, was in his sixth year in

University of Louisville Sports Information

Reece Gaines looks for an opening.

Lexington. Before a crowd of 20,061, Pitino, who was 6-2 against U of L as the UK coach, posted his first win for the Cards over the Cats, 81-63, and avenged the previous season's loss in Rupp.

J. Breck Smither/University of Kentucky Audio-Visual Archives
Tubby Smith and Rick Pitino

The teams' next game in Freedom Hall came on December 28, 2004, and it turned out to be as controversial as it was thrilling. With U of L leading 58-57 and time running out, UK's Patrick Sparks drove to the basket. Cut off on the baseline and in trouble, the junior guard quickly called timeout with 4.8 seconds remaining.

When play resumed, Sparks inbounded the ball to Kelenna Azubuike, who took two dribbles before throwing it back to Sparks, wide-open in the corner. Sparks set his feet behind the three-point line, and, with U of L's Ellis Myles rushing at him, he pump-faked Myles off his feet and jumped right, drawing contact with the flying Myles.

The officials called Myles for the foul and awarded Sparks three shots as the crowd of 20,088 went bonkers. As the officials discussed how many seconds to put on the clock, Coach Smith called Sparks to the sideline to settle him down. "Where are you going for Christmas?" Smith said. "Going home," said Sparks, who then returned to the foul line.

An 85 per cent free-throw shooter, Sparks swished all three to give the Cats a 60-58 victory. That was one of only five losses the Cards suffered in a 33-win season that didn't end until Illinois beat them in the Final Four in St. Louis. That trip made Pitino the first coach to take three different programs – Providence, UK and U of L – to the Big Show.

Two years later, although nobody knew it at the time,

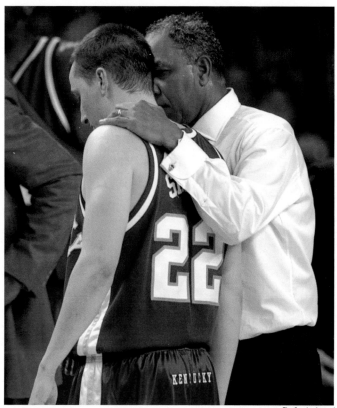

The Courier-Journal
Tubby Smith gets Patrick Sparks to loosen up before his game-winning free throws in 2004.

Smith coached his final game against U of L as the UK head coach when the teams met on December 16, 2006, in Freedom Hall. Both teams were young and struggling, UK coming into the game with a 7-3 record to U of L's 5-4.

The Cards started strong, leading by as much as seven in the early going, but the Cats came back to take a 17-16 lead on Luke Obrzut's bucket with 6:04 to play. With 1:40 to go, freshman Mike Porter drilled a three-pointer on an assist from fellow freshman Jodie Meeks and UK never again trailed on the way to a workmanlike 61-49 victory. In ten games against the Cards, Smith was 6-4.

After the season, Smith shocked the hoops world by announcing that he was leaving UK to take the Minnesota job. His replacement was Billy Clyde Gillispie, the Texas A&M coach whose team had eliminated the Cards from the 2007 NCAA tournament with a 72-69 upset in Rupp Arena, of all places. Some fans insisted then, and still do, that the main reason UK hired Gillispie was that win over Pitino on the Cats' home floor.

The Courier-Journal
U of L's Edgar Sosa hit a game-winning three against the Cats on January 4, 2009.

The Courier-Journal
Sosa celebrated the Cards' narrow escape.

On January 4, 2009, Gillispie coached his second and last game against the Cards as the Cats' head coach. The previous year, the Cards posted an 89-75 win in Rupp that dropped Gillispie's first UK team to 6-7. The Cats rallied for an 18-13 record that got them into the NCAA tournament.

But Gillispie's second team came into Freedom Hall with an 11-3 record and hopes of an upset against a U of L team that had so far failed to live up to its No. 3 pre-season ranking. In its previous game, the Cards had been upset in Freedom Hall by lowly UNLV. Pitino was so upset with junior point guard Edgar Sosa that he benched him and told him, "If I were you, I'd transfer."

University of Louisville Sports Information

Every Cats-Cards game in Freedom Hall drew a standing-room-only crowd.

Gillispie remembered Sosa well from the 2007 NCAA game in Rupp Arena. He laid 31 points on Texas A&M that day, but missed a long three at the end that would have tied it for the Cards. This time Sosa broke out of his slump with an 18-point effort that included the game-winning shot, a deep three with 2.6 left in the game. It was virtually the same shot he had missed in 2007.

"I knew Sosa wasn't going to pass it," Gillispie said. "He killed us when he played us two years ago. He wanted to take that last shot and that's probably why he made it."

Of all the radio shows upon which that game was analyzed, the most unlikely was the one co-hosted by a couple of coaches who once hated each other with a passion. Incredibly to anyone who remembered the acrimony of the late 1970s and early '80s, Joe B. Hall and Denny Crum agreed to team up five days a week for a show that was syndicated around the state and proved to be remarkably popular.

Which just goes to prove that the only thing anybody knows for sure about the UK-U of L rivalry is, well, you never know.

AFTERWORD

The University of Louisville's last season in Freedom Hall got off to a routine start. The Cards defeated an NAIA school, Georgetown College, and an NCAA Division II program, Bellarmine College (coached by former U of L assistant Scotty Davenport), in exhibition play, then began their 54th regular season with victories over East Tennessee State, Morgan State, and Appalachian State.

But controversy reared its familiar head on November 28, when Coach John Calipari brought his first Kentucky team into Freedom Hall for a public practice session before their November 30 game against UNC-Asheville. Toward the end of the session, which was attended by an estimated 3,000 blue-clad fans, star UK forward Patrick Patterson heard a fan yell, "Patrick, jump on the Cardinal!"

And so he did, stomping on the U of L logo that's emblazoned on the Freedom Hall court. Following their leader, two more UK players – sophomore Josh Harrelson and freshman DeMarcus Cousins – then joined in, leaping simultaneously and coming down on the bird-head logo with both feet.

Freshman point guard John Wall was about to join in the fun when Wildcat assistant coach Orlando Antigua broke it up, waving a finger of admonishment. "It's kind of good that our coach stopped us," said Wall, "so we wouldn't start no kind of battle or beef with them."

Oh, no. Heaven forbid that UK would start a beef with U of L. Whatever courses Wall was taking in the first

University of Kentucky Audio-Visual Archives
UK Coach John Calipari

semester of what was expected to be a one-and-done career in Lexington, hoops history was not one of them. But he can be forgiven on the grounds that he was several years from being born when the UK-U of L regular-season rivalry began in 1983.

At the time of the bird-stomping, the Cardinals were in Las Vegas to play the Runnin' Rebels. They lost that game, their first of the season, and then returned home to beat Stetson on December 2. But then they were upset twice in a row in Freedom Hall – a rare occurrence – by UNC-Charlotte and Western Carolina before gathering themselves to run off consecutive wins over Oral Roberts, Western Kentucky, Louisiana-Lafayette, Radford and South Florida to close out the 2009 portion of the season.

By the time of the 73-52 win over South Florida on December 30, various commercial outlets around the city were doing a brisk business in T-shirts, caps, and sweatshirts that commemorated the Cards' last season in Freedom Hall. Moreover, the tickets to each home game featured a Cardinal star from the past. For the South Florida game, it was Charlie Tyra, the 6-8 rebounding and scoring demon who was a senior in 1956-'57, the year the Cards moved into Freedom Hall on a part-time basis.

"I was there the night Charlie laid 40 on Notre Dame (December 22, 1956)," said Al Benninger, a press-table fixture at Freedom Hall. "I'll never forget it because it was the same day I moved into my new house at 3121 Maywood. Imagine that. Me and U of L moving into new homes at the same time."

Everybody has a favorite Freedom Hall memory. Or two or three or too many to talk about in a mere book. But the night of the South Florida game, two games kept popping up in a brief survey of Freedom Hall veterans.

The first was U of L's 70-69 win over Memphis on March 2, 1986.

"We were down by a point with only seconds remaining and Andre Turner, their best free-throw shooter, was going to the line," said Kenny Klein, U of L's sports information director since 1983. "The atmosphere was complete dejection because, in those days before the three-point shot, there seemed to be no way we could win. But Turner missed, a miracle in itself, and Billy Thompson got the rebound for us. Milt Wagner got the ball for us and darned

if Turner didn't foul him on the baseline.

"The crowd went from being completely deflated to going crazy because they knew Milt wouldn't miss the free throws because he was so cool under pressure. He made the first one and then motioned for the crowd to turn up the noise. I couldn't believe it. Then he made the second one to give us the win. I went out to grab Milt and got soaked with a beer."

The second was Marquette's double-overtime 80-79 victory over the Cardinals on February 28, 1996.

"As soon as the game is over, the Marquette coach, Mike Deane, runs to the middle of the floor and gives the crowd the finger," said Steve Thompson, a former captain with the Louisville Metro Police. "As you can imagine, the crowd went nuts. It was like the Little Big Horn out there. Whatever the fans could throw, they threw – beer, coffee, coins, you name it."

"I went up to the Marquette athletics director," said Joe Lampkin, also a Louisville policeman, "and said, 'You better get him out of here now.' When we finally got Deane back to the locker room, he said, 'I didn't do anything.' I told him, 'Man, it was on national TV…you were lucky you weren't killed."

U of L coaches didn't have police protection until 1974.

"I guess Denny Crum didn't feel comfortable about having non-police security," said Thompson. "So he called me in one day to talk about it. I thought he had the wrong Thompson – I was only a patrolman in those days – but he said he wanted me to get five other guys to provide security at games.

"He told me the only problem was that there wasn't any

money in the budget for it at that time, so we worked out a deal: In exchange for providing security, the university would give us each four tickets for home games and take two of us on road trips. That was fine with us. I always picked the road trips to Florida State, because I knew Denny would want to go fishing, and to New Orleans, because I knew there was a good chance we'd hit the casinos."

University of Louisville Sports Information

Maestro Denny Crum "conducted" Cardinal games for over 30 years with his trademark rolled-up program.

Sticking close to Crum for more than 25 years earned Thompson so much TV time that his envious buddies on the force began calling him "Hollywood Steve." After Crum retired, Thompson removed himself from being the coach's personal bodyguard and turned the job over to his son, Dale, also a Metro policeman. To this day Dale serves Rick Pitino in the same capacity his dad served Crum.

The duty isn't always easy.

"I remember fans cussing Crum as he walked up the tunnel ramp after his last game," said Zack Hardin. "And I remember before one game a fan yelling at Pitino, 'Why don't you get a real job?' Rick just looked at him and smiled and said, 'You have a nice day.' After that, they put up barricades to keep the fans away from the players and coaches as much as possible."

For three years, Hardin has been the man in charge of the media and players' door at the rear of Freedom Hall. This is the entrance that always has been blocked off to fans. In 54 years, just about every great coach, player, and entertainer in the nation has walked through that door at one time or another. And, of course, there have been times when police had to escort misbehaving fans out the door.

"One time the Grateful Dead had concerts here two days in a row," says Steve Thompson. "I've never seen so many stoned people in my life. They brought in kinds of dope I hadn't seen in years – peyote, mescaline, nitrous oxide. We locked up 268 over the two days. There were so many we had to use the horse chutes behind the building. We'd chain 'em to the fence until the next booking van came along to take them downtown."

Courier-Journal photographer Bill Luster, who probably holds the Freedom Hall record for most events photographed, recalls a time when Neil Leifer, the celebrity photographer from *Sports Illustrated*, got arrested after getting into a beef with Freedom Hall security about a camera position. Leifer pioneered the concept of putting a camera directly over a backboard.

Not unreasonably, the authorities might have feared that Leifer would fall through the roof and splatter himself on the floor. That almost happened, believe it or not, during a Kentucky Colonels game. Apparently some kids got drunk and decided it would be a good idea to explore the catwalks over the ceiling. One of them fell through the roof and landed in the lower-level seats. Amazingly, he survived.

Everybody has a Freedom Hall memory.

Ed Peak, veteran freelance sports writer: "The year after Wes Unseld graduated, I remember buying a $1 ticket from a Convenient store and sitting in an aisle for my first U of L game."

Jody Demling, *Courier-Journal* sports writer: "My uncle, Leo Ghafer, took me to watch the finals of the 1988 boys state tournament. We sat up in section 341. That was the night Richie Farmer and Allan Houston went at it. I'm told it was the greatest high school game ever in Freedom Hall."

Steve Thompson: "I handled the police security for concerts, and one night Hank Williams, Jr. came out and poured a quart of Jack Daniels into the crowd. Then he sang something like, 'Let's get rowdy!' and the crowd felt an obligation to do just that."

J.T. Cosdon, local rock 'n' roll legend: "I'll never forget the night I saw Roy Orbison in Freedom Hall. He was the best."

Russ Brown, longtime writer for The Courier-Journal and the *Louisville Sports Report*: "The Eagles put on a great concert a few years ago, and I'll never forget Cher the night she performed here on a farewell tour that turned out to be not a farewell tour after all."

Ken Horn, statistician and former U of L publicity assistant: "The night that Denny Crum got his 600th win, I was cleaning up the press table and I noticed that Coach Crum

Billy Joel and Elton John: dueling pianos in Freedom Hall.

had left his rolled-up program laying there. I picked it up and took it to him in case he wanted to keep it. I also thought the Billy Joel-Elton John concert was something special."

Dr. John Ellis, U of L team doctor and son of Rudy Ellis, who served in that capacity for decades: "I played here on the U of L freshman team and I'll never forget hitting my first shot from the top of the key and hearing John Tong say, 'Goaaalll by Ellis!' I also came here for the circus in the third grade and noticed I couldn't see too well when I looked up at the scoreboard. That's when I knew I needed glasses."

Kenny Klein: "There's nothing like the sound of the crowd in Freedom Hall when we get a run going against a good team. I remember a game against North Carolina (December 18, 1999) when they were ranked No. 6. I remember that Marques Maybin, Nate Johnson, and Reece Gaines got this run going just before halftime that was unbelievable: Dunks followed by steals followed by more dunks. It just got deafening in here – as loud as it's ever been. To me, times like that are when Freedom Hall was at its best."

The Cards last eight games in Freedom Hall included some contests against foes who have a special place in U of L hoops history, most notably Cincinnati and Notre Dame.

Darrell Griffith's No. 35 was retired.

The most fitting final opponent would have been Memphis, the team Cards fans love most to beat that's not named UK. However, that honor went to Syracuse, which came to town for a 2 p.m. game on Saturday, March 6.

Freedom's reign as one of the nation's premier multi-purpose arenas will not end when the lights are turned out after the final U of L game. But without the Cards as its main tenant, the building will take on a new identity, both locally and nationally. The next time UK plays in Freedom Hall, for example, there will be no stomping on the bird because the bird will be gone.

But the ghosts will remain forever.

Will it ever be possible to stand in Freedom Hall without hearing the voice of John Tong? Without seeing Denny Crum patrolling the sideline, jaws working furiously on a piece of gum and rolled-up program in hand? Without hearing the roar that always came when Wes Unseld ripped off a rebound or Darrell Griffith threw down a slam?

Of course not. But there's still this: As soon as the last U of L game is done, the Freedom Hall workers will take up the floor to make room for the circus or a concert or whatever else is coming next. The Cards are changing their home address, but the building will still be around for a new generation of heroes and dreamers.

KENTUCKY STATE FAIR BOARD MEMBERS

(CURRENT)

Steven L. Beshear

Governor

Lanny Greer

Chairman
Manchester

Ronald Carmicle

Vice Chairman
Louisville

Harold Workman

President & CEO
Kentucky State Fair Board

Richie Farmer

Commisioner of Kentucky
Department of Agriculture

Marcheta Sparrow

Governor's Representative
Tourism, Arts & Heritage Secretary
Commonwealth of Kentucky

Dr. M. Scott Smith

Dean of the University of Kentucky
College of Agriculture

Jane Cave

Glendale
Kentucky

Gib Gosser

Somerset

KENTUCKY STATE FAIR BOARD MEMBERS

(CURRENT)

Hilda Legg

Somerset

Mike Libs

Philpot

William Malone

Louisville

Sam Moore

Morgantown

Fred Sarver

Paris

Thomas Schifano

Louisville

William Tolle

Maysville

Steve Wilson

Goshen

KENTUCKY STATE FAIR BOARD MEMBERS

(1950-PRESENT)

BOARD CHAIRS

Smith D. Broadbent, Jr. (1952-1959)

H.G. Whittenberg, Sr. (1959-1960)

F. W. Curran (1960-1965)

E. Galloday LaMotte (1965-1968)

Douglas Blair (1968-1972)

Wyndall Smith (1972-1980)

William G. Earley (1980)

Joseph E. Stopher (1980-1981)

Charles A. Hertzman (1981-1984)

Clarence Duggins, Jr. (1984-1988)

Joe Claxon (1988-1989)

Daniel C. Ulmer, Jr. (1989-1995)

William Kuegel (1995-2001)

Mary Anne Cronan (2001-2004)

Thomas Schifano (2006-2008)

Lanny Greer (2004-2006; 2008-present)

GOVERNORS

Lawrence W. Wetherby (1950-1955)

Albert B. "Happy" Chandler (1955-1959)

Bert T. Combs (1959-1963)

Edward "Ned" Breathitt (1963-1967)

Louie B. Nunn (1967-1971)

Wendall H. Ford (1971-1974)

Julian M. Carroll (1974-1979)

John Y. Brown, Jr. (1979-1983)

Martha Layne Collins (1983-1987)

Wallace Wilkinson (1987-1991)

Brereton C. Jones (1991-1995)

Paul E. Patton (1995-2003)

Ernie Fletcher, M.D. (2003-2007)

Steven L. Beshear (2007 – Present)

LIEUTENANT GOVERNORS

Emerson Beauchamp (1951-1954)

Harry Lee Waterfield (1955-1958; 1964-1967)

Wilson Wyatt (1959-1963)

Wendall H. Ford (1968-1971)

Julian M. Carroll (1972-1975)

Thelma Stovall (1976-1979)

Martha Layne Collins (1980-1983)

Steven L. Beshear (1984-1987)

Brereton Jones (1988-1991)

Paul Patton (1992-1995)

Stephen L. Henry, M.D. (1996-2003)

Steve Pence (2004-2007)

Daniel Mongiardo, M.D. (2007-Present)

KENTUCKY STATE FAIR BOARD MEMBERS

(1950-PRESENT)

BOARD MEMBERS

Andrew "Skipper" Martin

Anna Jane Cave

Arthur G. Meyer

Arthur H. Raderer

B.C. Colton

Ben L. Cowgill

Bruce D. Harper

Dr. C. Oran Little

Capt. James R. Rash

Carl Dohn

Dr. Charles Barnhart

Charles E. Eastin D.V.M.

Charles L. Hamilton

Charles A. Hertzman

Clarence Duggins, Jr.

Crit Luallen

Daniel C. Ulmer, Jr.

Daniel D. Briscoe

Daniel Reed

David V. Hall

Derrick Ramsey

Don L. Johnston

Douglas L. Blair

E. Galloday LaMotte

Ed Logsdon

Edwin Sutton

F.W. Curran

Frank Schadler, Jr.

Frank Welch

Fred K. Sarver

GeorgeE. Clark

George F. Kinkead

George Stiles

Gib Gosser

H.G. Whittenberg, Sr.

Harry Lee Waterfield II

Hayward Spinks

Hilda G. Legg

Ivan Jett

J. R. Sanderlin

J. Robert Miller

Jacob Graves

James S. Karp

Janie Bruce

Jerry Pace

James W. Ellis

Joe Claxon

Joe Wright

John Fred Williams

KENTUCKY STATE FAIR BOARD MEMBERS

(1950-PRESENT)

John L. Knopf, Sr.

Joseph E. Stopher, Sr.

Joseph R. Bell

Lanny Greer

Lucian Isbell

Luther House

Dr. M. Scott Smith

Malcolm B. Chancey, Jr.

Marcheta Sparrow

Mary Kate Kordes

Max Ladt

Mike Libs

Mrs. James E. Bruce

Mrs. Wyndall Smith (Piny Smith)

Philip W. Bale, M.D.

R. Eric Waldman

Rita Y. Phillips

Robert C. Crosby

Robert Heady

Robert A. Kalb

Robert L. Wilson

Robinson S. Brown, Jr.

Ronald L. Carmicle

Roy Stevens

Russell L. Salsman

Sam Moore

Steve Wilson

Tandy Carol Patrick

Thomas T. Ladt

Thomas J. Schifano

W. James Host

Ward "Butch" Burnette

Dr. William A. Seay

William Earley

William M. Kuegel, Sr.

William P. Malone

William Stone

William B. Tolle

Wyndall Smith

COMMISSIONERS OF AGRICULTURE

Ben S. Adams (1951-1954)

Ben J. Butler (1955-1958)

Emerson Beauchamp (1959-1963)

Wendall P. Butler (1964-1967; 1972-1975)

J. Robert Miller (1968-1971)

Thomas O. Harris (1976-1979)

Alben W. Barkley II (1980-1983)

David Boswell (1984-1987)

Ward "Butch" Burnette (1988-1991)

Ed Logsdon (1992-1995)

Billy Ray Smith (1996-2003)

Richie Farmer (2004-Present)